101 Language Games
for Children

Other SmartFun Books

101 Music Games for Children by Jerry Storms

101 More Music Games for Children by Jerry Storms

101 Drama Games for Children by Paul Rooyackers

101 More Drama Games for Children by Paul Rooyackers

101 Dance Games for Children by Paul Rooyackers

101 Movement Games for Children by Huberta Wiertsema

Coming Soon:

101 More Dance Games for Children by Paul Rooyackers

Yoga Games for Children by Danielle Bersma and Marjoke Visscher

Ordering

Trade bookstores in the U.S. and Canada, please contact:

Publishers Group West
1700 Fourth Street, Berkeley CA 94710
Phone: (800) 788-3123 Fax: (510) 528-3444

Hunter House books are available at bulk discounts for course adoptions;
to qualifying community, health-care, and government organizations;
and for special promotions and fund-raising. For details please contact:

Special Sales Department
Hunter House Inc., PO Box 2914, Alameda CA 94501-0914
Phone: (510) 865-5282 Fax: (510) 865-4295
E-mail: ordering@hunterhouse.com

Individuals can order our books from most bookstores,
by calling **(800) 266-5592**, or from our
website at **www.hunterhouse.com**

101
Language Games
FOR
Children

Fun and Learning with Words,
Stories, and Poems

Paul Rooyackers

Translated by Amina Marix Evans

a Hunter House SmartFun book

Hunter House Inc., Publishers
PO Box 2914
Alameda CA 94501-0914

Library of Congress Cataloging-in-Publication Data
Rooyackers, Paul.
    [Honderd taalspelen. English]
    101 language games for children : fun and learning with words, stories,
and poems / by Paul Rooyackers ; translated by Amina Marix Evans.
        p. cm. — (A Hunter House smartfun book)
    Translated from Dutch.
    Includes index.
    ISBN 0-89793-369-9 (pbk.) — ISBN 0-89793-370-2 (spiral bound)
    1. Language arts (Elementary)—Activity programs. 2. Language arts
(Secondary)—Activity programs. 3. Literary recreations. I. Title: One
hundred one language games for children. II. Title: One hundred and one
language games for children. III. Title. IV. Series.
LB1576 .R67513 2002
372.6044—dc21   2002012400

Project Credits

Cover Design and Book Production:
  Jil Weil

Book Design: Hunter House

Developmental and Copy Editor:
  Ashley Chase

Proofreader: John David Marion

Acquisitions Editor: Jeanne Brondino

Editor: Alexandra Mummery

Publisher: Kiran S. Rana

Publicity Coordinator:
  Earlita K. Chenault

Sales & Marketing Coordinator:
  JoAnne Retzlaff

Customer Service Manager:
  Christina Sverdrup

Order Fulfillment: Lakdhon Lama

Administrator: Theresa Nelson

Computer Support: Peter Eichelberger

Printed and Bound by Bang Printing, Brainerd, Minnesota

Manufactured in the United States of America
9 8 7 6 5 4 3 2 1   First Edition   02 03 04 05 06

Co_children : fun and learning

*A detailed list of the games indicating
appropriate age groups begins on the next page.*

List of Games

List of Games, continued

List of Games, continued

List of Games, continued

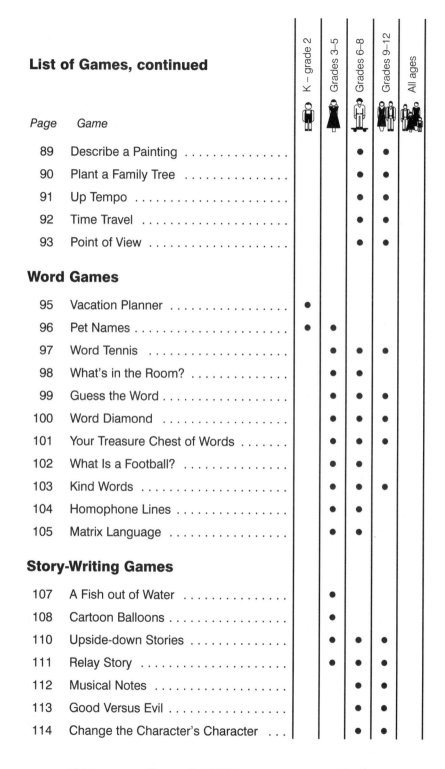

List of Games, continued

Preface

Language is immensely powerful, but it can also be loads of fun. In fact, a sense of fun can make language more powerful—witness the wordplay of Shakespeare and the rhyming patterns of orators and preachers like Jesse Jackson. Language and play complement and enrich each other. A fusion of the two produces language games, the subject of this book.

This book contains over one hundred language games and variations, as well as an introduction that explains how the games can be made accessible to everyone. All the language games have been carefully developed and tested in a classroom setting. You do not need a great deal of experience to lead the games, but do review and rehearse them carefully before you introduce them to players.

The language games can be used in schools, writing groups, storytelling workshops, and many other contexts. Within the field of education, they are particularly applicable to language arts, English, creative writing, poetry, drama, and public speaking classes.

Best of luck!

Paul Rooyackers
The Netherlands

For easy reading, we have alternated use of the male and female pronouns. Of course, every "he" also means "she," and vice versa!

Introduction

Objectives

The language games in this book serve various educational goals applicable to language arts, English, creative writing, poetry, drama, and public speaking classes. They are also valuable to players' personal and social development. The games are designed to:

- **encourage appreciation for language**
  "I can't write." "I don't have anything to say." Many kids find writing and public speaking intimidating. They feel they can't express themselves well, so they don't like trying. The games included in this book invite kids to play with words, expressions, and stories. Players express themselves in an ungraded, noncompetitive environment. The games show kids that using language can be fun.

- **foster creativity**
  This sense of fun helps unlock players' creativity. Writing or speaking becomes a game of make-believe instead of a chore. The structure of the games also encourages creativity. Faced with an open-ended assignment, many kids find their minds as blank as the sheet of paper (or the faces of the audience) in front of them. It can be very difficult to come up with ideas out of nowhere. These games give players a framework on which to hang their ideas. Still, they leave plenty of room for imagination and innovation. Many games encourage players

to look at words, subjects, and stories from a new angle. New perspectives lead to unexpected ideas.

- **increase vocabulary**
Playing with new words is one of the best ways to become familiar with them. These games give players opportunities to collect words, create word associations, think about the sounds of words and the sensory impressions they evoke, and become familiar and comfortable with new words from clues about their meaning or context.

- **develop fluency**
These games encourage players to write and speak freely, developing ease in using language. Language games challenge players to experiment with new words and different ways of speaking and expressing themselves. By turns, players are encouraged to think about words and to use words spontaneously. This combination of activities helps children learn to choose words both more easily and more precisely. Players find their voices by using them.

- **develop understanding of composition and story structure**
Making up a story that will engage an audience is no easy task. The storytelling and writing games let players explore story structure and the various elements of a story: plot, character, and so on. Players come to understand what makes a story interesting and how compelling stories are constructed.

- **improve public speaking skills**
These games provide many opportunities to practice speaking in a supportive environment. Various games involve group discussions, dialogs, reading aloud, and storytelling. Players learn to use tone of voice, emphasis, tempo, and volume to engage their listeners. Other games invite players to have fun with their voices, making funny sounds, being noisy, and experimenting. Players develop ease in vocalizing and overcome barriers of shyness and stage fright.

- **develop social skills: self-expression, listening, collaborating**
Language games expand players' powers of communication, both as speakers and as listeners. Players learn how to express

themselves in a group and how others react to them. As others read aloud, tell stories, and make presentations, players practice listening with respect and reacting honestly but constructively. The games also give players ample opportunities to work in pairs, in small groups, and as a class. They provide practice in collaborating, making decisions together, and inviting contributions from each group member in turn. Expressing themselves through language games will help players build self-confidence as well as tolerance for other points of view.

Information for the Leader

The leader plays many important roles in conducting these language games: organizer, stage manager, debate moderator, master of ceremonies, cheerleader, and more. As leader, be sure to:

- **Prepare the space.** It is important that the workspace is pleasant and comfortable to speak, listen, discuss, and write in. A room without too many distractions—noise from outside, excessive decoration, and so on—is ideal. The arrangement of the tables can help create an open, inviting atmosphere. A traditional classroom setup with desks in rows facing front can feel stifling. A circle or square of desks invites interaction and play.

- **Prepare the necessary materials.** Players and a sense of fun are all that are needed for many of the games. Other games require newspapers, art supplies, audiovisual equipment, and such materials. Check the Materials heading ahead of time and make sure you have everything you will need.

- **Prepare yourself.** Try out each language game yourself before using it with a group. Think about how best to present a particular game to a particular group. Plan out in advance how to explain the game, making sure that your instructions are not too complicated. Visualize the way the game will develop and think about where problems could arise. Always have a "plan B" up your sleeve just in case your original plan cannot be used for some reason. You may, for instance, have planned for a group of thirty people but suddenly have to cope with far more or fewer participants. In this case, some language games—such as game 89 (Relay Story)—could turn out to be much less fun.

- **Talk the players through the game.** Take special care with your introduction of a game. If the players have not heard and understood the assignment properly, the results are doomed from the outset. Communicate your enthusiasm and interest to the players through your tone of voice. Provide ideas and encouragement as the game goes on. If the game is taking off in the wrong direction, guide it back on course with constructive suggestions. Round off the game with a discussion or performance.

- **Create an open, supportive atmosphere.** When we express ourselves, we often feel vulnerable. A player reading a poem that voices his personal thoughts and feelings needs to do so in a safe environment. Creating such an environment is your most important duty as leader. Your constructive remarks and suggestions about players' work will set the tone. Above all, you should make an agreement within the group that no one will make negative comments about the way others perform their assignments. Writing or telling a story is a voluntary activity; no one can be forced into this form of expression. If players resist activities such as reading aloud, don't put too much pressure on them. A relaxed atmosphere should eventually make all concerned feel comfortable enough to express themselves. Reading what is happening, listening closely to the remarks of the participants, and being sensitive to the group's feelings are all part of the leader's task.

- **Give players plenty of feedback about their progress.** Communication requires an audience. Every member of the group will value your comments, suggestions, and encouragement. Give players your attention. Read their texts, listen to their stories, and watch them as they play the games. If you feel that someone's speaking or writing has improved, that she is listening or reacting better than before—tell her! This personal approach is vital, but so is encouraging a spirit of cooperation. Throwing twenty or thirty people together in a room does not mean that they will automatically form a cohesive group. Point out instances when the group has worked together well. Make suggestions of ways to incorporate individual players' strengths in group projects. Focus not only on personal achievement, but also on the development of the group's work as a whole.

- **Tailor the activities to the group.** How large is your group? How old are the players? How mature are they? How proficient are they at writing or speaking? How motivated are they? Do they have experience with expressing their feelings, speaking in public, reading to a group, or being vulnerable in the face of other people? You need to know where the group members excel and what their weak points are. Adjust the activities to the players' level of proficiency, so that they will not become frustrated or bored. For example, young children can't do writing activities, but they can make letter collages. The List of Games on pages vi through x includes a chart showing at a glance the appropriate age level for each game. See the Key to the Icons Used in the Games, page 10, for more information on the age levels.

Pay special attention to those who have previously regarded language as a deadly serious and terrifying subject. Do all the participants have the confidence to express themselves? Are there some people in the group who stutter or stammer or who are dyslexic? Some people find it very hard to express themselves in words or cannot bear to read out loud. Take extra care with these players to make sure the games remain fun and not an ordeal.

Information about the Games

The one hundred and one language games in this book are divided into the following nine categories. Each category begins with brief information about the characteristics of the games in that group. Within each section, the games progress roughly from the simplest to the most complex:

- letter games

- newspaper games

- sensory games

- introduction games

- sound games

- storytelling games

- word games

- story-writing games

- poetry games

About Exercises and Games (Letter Games, Newspaper Games, Sensory Games, Introduction Games, Sound Games, and Word Games)

Many of the games in this book invite players to explore language without the pressure of creating a finished product such as a story or poem. These games are terrific for building vocabulary and other language skills. They can also be used for gathering ideas that players can develop into a finished piece later.

About Composing Stories (Story-Writing Games and Storytelling Games)

A story is more than a series of events. Without a carefully built structure, even the most sensational happenings will not engage an audience. The story games allow players to explore composition and discover what goes into the creation and development of an engrossing story. The following paragraphs provide suggestions on how to walk a group through the steps of creating a story.

There are six major elements that make up a story:

- theme (a story's "message" or moral)

- characters (who the story is about)

- setting (where and when the story takes place)

- conflict (the main problem the characters try to solve)

- plot (the events that take place)

- resolution (the solution to the problem—or a conclusion that does not solve the problem, but still gives the audience a feeling of closure)

Invite players to work together to make up a story. Depending on their ages, ask volunteers to note down the group's ideas on the chalkboard, or do so yourself. You might have players decide on a **theme** at the outset, or you might allow the theme to emerge as the story takes shape. Have players begin with one or two main **characters**—the hero(es) of the story. Ask: Who are they? What are their personalities like? What are their hopes and fears? Where do they live? This leads into the story's **setting.** Have players decide on a time and place (real or imaginary) in which the story takes place.

Now for the most important part: the **conflict.** To create an interesting story, it is essential to build tension. Ask the group to think of a problem the characters face. Is there a villain who threatens them? Do they have a secret wish that cannot be fulfilled without great hardship? This conflict will be the stimulus that makes everything happen. Ask: How does the problem affect the characters? How will they try to solve it? What happens as a result of their attempts to solve it?

From all this a **plot** develops. Encourage players to think of complications that stand in the way of solving the main conflict and create twists and turns in the plot. Then have them decide on a **resolution.** Ask: Do the characters solve their problem? How will the story end? Point out that a resolution does not have to be a happy one: Perhaps the conflict simply cannot be solved. They should, however, give the audience some sort of closure: if not a solution, then an important event or new understanding that rounds off the story. As players develop the plot, have them note additional characters who play supporting roles. Players should describe the characters and how they are related to each other. All of the information about the story is noted on the board so that everyone can see and decide together whether certain roles or episodes should be scrapped, and whether anything needs to be added.

Now players can put these elements together to form a story. They might work in groups to write it down, or they might take turns telling it orally. As we all know, every story has three parts:

- beginning

- middle

- end

The story's **beginning** introduces the setting and the main characters. The audience learns about the characters' personalities, situations, and relationships. In the beginning of the story, the conflict makes its first appearance. This problem changes everything: The situation described at the outset can no longer exist and the story is set into motion.

In the story's **middle**, the characters attempt to solve the conflict. Their actions have various results, and other events may occur to complicate their attempts at a solution. Heroes and villains may show their true colors. The events of the plot lead up to a climax—an especially exciting event that is the decisive moment in resolving the conflict. At the **end** of the story, we see how the resolution has affected the characters.

Tell players that it is important to plan a story's end before telling its beginning. They must know how the story will end in order to show how the conflict arises and the resolution develops. A story's end makes a great difference to its beginning.

About Telling Stories (Storytelling Games)

Storytelling is an art that can only be mastered through practice. Storytellers must learn to observe—everyday observations can form the basis for great storytelling material. Many stories grow from events that have happened in the storyteller's own life. Storytellers also need to develop their memories: They must be able to remember an entire story before they can tell it. And, of course, storytellers must use their voices to engage the audience, to act the parts of different characters and show their moods, and to communicate the excitement of a climax. The storytelling games let players explore the special skills involved in telling an engrossing story.

If you have little experience with storytelling, you may want to practice on your own before introducing storytelling games to a group. You might record your story so that you can hear for yourself how it sounds. You may also want to try out a story by telling it to a friend or two. That way you can see the reaction of a live audience.

About Writing Poems (Poetry Games)

Stories are about what happened. Poems are about translating impressions and feelings into words. The poetry games help players gather their thoughts and give players some structure to help them express themselves. Many of the other language games could be adapted to result in a poem as well. Players' poems could involve rhythm or rhyme, but this is not necessary. These games are not designed to produce literary gems; they are simply a way of playing with language. We hope that through the use of the poetry games in this book such preconceptions as "Poetry is silly," "I can't write a good poem," or "My feelings aren't that interesting" will disappear.

How to Combine Games to Form a Comprehensive Program

These games may be used to supplement a traditional language arts curriculum. They may also be used as the core of a creative writing or storytelling program. In the latter case, you can give each class session a logical structure by choosing games to serve various functions. Sports teams first warm up, then play a game, and end with a debriefing. You can give your classes a similar structure. A class lasting an hour requires an introduction of about 15 minutes, a main activity of about 30 minutes, and a further 15 minutes for rounding-off.

The Introduction

In the first phase of the session the players break free from their daily reality and tune in to the atmosphere of the game(s) they will be playing. Sensory games are particularly well suited for waking the class up and developing concentration. The introductory activity may also generate ideas that form the basis for the core activity. For example, a word list or association exercise could lead to a written text on a particular theme. See below for specific examples.

The Core Activity

At this point the group tackles the main activity you have chosen for it. The players might speak, listen, narrate, or write. Now the purpose of the session becomes clear. As the leader, set a goal for yourself that can be worked out during this phase.

Processing or Presentation

In the final phase the group may present their work by reading aloud, telling stories, or displaying letter collages or other creations.

Alternatively, you might have the group members share their experiences of the core activity in a discussion.

Example: Begin with an association game that leads into a storytelling game and end the session with a 60-second report from each participant.

Games that could lead to stories:

- game 15 (Clipping the Headlines)
- game 19 (Photo Finish)
- game 23 (A Newspaper Story)
- game 31 (When I Grow Up...)
- game 46 (A Noise in the Dark)
- game 55 (Sound and Fury Signifying Something)

Games that could lead to poems:

- game 29 (I Hear the Waves Crashing)
- game 30 (The Sound of Words)
- game 34 (Do You Like Liver?)
- game 36 (Nice to Meet You)
- game 37 (My Favorite Word)
- game 54 (What Sounds Do You See?)
- game 80 (Word Diamond)
- game 81 (Your Treasure Chest of Words)

Key to the Icons Used with the Games

To help you find games suitable for a particular situation, all the games are coded with symbols or icons. These icons tell you at a glance the following things about each game:

- the appropriate grade level/age group

- the amount of time needed

- the organization of the players

- the materials required

- the space required

These are explained in more detail below.

Suitability in terms of age The age groups correspond to grade level divisions commonly used in the educational system:

= Young children in kindergarten through grade 2 (ages 4 through 8)

= Older children in grades 3 through 5 (ages 8 through 11)

= Adolescents in middle school, grades 6 through 8 (ages 11 through 14)

= Teenagers in high school, grades 9 through 12 (ages 14 through 18)

= All ages

How long the game takes The games are divided into those that require about 10 minutes, 15 minutes, 20 minutes, 30 minutes, 40 minutes or more, and those that require multiple class sessions.

10 minutes

15 minutes

20 minutes

30 minutes

40 minutes or more

multiple sessions

The organization of players All of the games can be adapted to virtually any size of group. The grouping icons indicate how players will be organized to play the game: in pairs, in small groups, as individuals, or all together as a group.

 – Players will work in pairs.

 – Players will work in small groups.

 – Players will work as individuals.

 – All the players will work together as a group.

Amount of space needed Nearly all of the games are best suited to a classroom setting. The games that require a large, gymnasium-sized space are marked with the following icon:

 – Large space needed

Whether you need materials Some games require the use of materials such as art supplies, newspapers, or audiovisual equipment. These games are flagged with the icon below, and the necessary materials are listed under the Materials heading. (It is assumed that basic classroom supplies such as writing paper, pens and pencils, and a chalkboard are readily available, and games requiring only these supplies are not flagged.)

 – Materials needed

Letter Games

How do children first discover letters? Through alphabet blocks and books, but also billboards, neon signs, street signs, food packaging, newspapers, magazines, plastic bags, money, T-shirts, alphabet soup.... Almost everywhere they look, kids see letters.

Letters not only appear everywhere, they also come in all shapes and sizes. They can take so many different forms—sometimes you can even eat them (the writing on a birthday cake) or smell them (the distinctive scent of a brand-new paperback). This series of games is a real adventure for children. It is a journey of discovery in Letterland.

To prepare for these games, gather old magazines and newspapers that can be cut up to create a "treasure chest" of letters.

Letter Collages

Materials: large sheets of paper; glue; safety scissors; old magazines and newspapers

Display the printed materials and point out that letters come in all sizes, shapes, and styles. Have children work individually or in twos or threes. Invite them to cut out any letters they like and glue them onto the sheets of paper. Encourage children to collect as many different letters of the alphabet as they can. Then have children display and compare their letter collages. Do some sheets have just black or white letters, or letters in one particular color or style, or are they all just a random jumble? Which letters of the alphabet do the children seem to like best, and why? Did anyone collect all 26 letters of the alphabet?

Variation: Which letters are neat, sloppy, plain, fancy, and so on? Have children describe the different styles of letters on their sheets.

Letter Hunt

Materials: a box full of pictures with text; a camera (optional)

In advance, search through magazines and picture books for pictures of letters used in the "real world"—on road signs, fire trucks, food packaging, and so on. Clip or flag the pictures, and collect them in a box. Then plan a short walk that will take children past all kinds of letters (for example, through a mall).

To begin the game, gather the children in a circle, display a number of pictures, and have children name the letters they see. Point out that letters come in all shapes and sizes and that they can be seen in many different places. After a few minutes, tell children that they are about to go out in search of letters. Guide children along your planned route, asking them to point out letters along the way. You may wish to photograph some of the letters for children to look at later.

Note: As it involves a walk in public, this game may require signed permission slips and/or arranging for additional chaperones. If this is not possible, you may wish to try the first variation listed below.

Variations:

- Instead of taking the children out, hang up or hide all sorts of different letters around the building—they can be upright, upside-down, or sideways. Have children search for letters and draw each one they find.

- This game could become a scavenger hunt. Divide the group into teams and assign a few specific letters for each team to find on your walk. Make sure to give each group a mix of common and unusual letters—for example, one team might have *e, k, s,* and *z* and another team *a, q, c,* and *t.*

Find the Letters

Materials: black-and-white photocopies of pictures with text; crayons or markers

See game 2 (Letter Hunt) for directions on collecting pictures with text. In advance, photocopy enough pictures from your collection so that every child can have one. Pass out the photocopies. Have children search for letters and color in each one they find. This game allows children to explore the forms of letters through play.

Variation: Hide the first letter of an object or an animal in a black-and-white drawing for children to color. For instance, you could draw a snake around an *s*.

Letterbox

Materials: old magazines and newspapers; small boxes; safety scissors; labels

Invite children to search through the newspapers and magazines for letters that catch their eye. As children search, they acquire an eye for form and style. Have them cut out any letters they like and collect them in several small boxes. As children begin filling the boxes, they can create (or dictate) labels telling what category of letter goes into each box. Children could create boxes for individual letters, or they might create more fanciful boxes, such as a box for noisy letters, a box for frilly letters, or a box for weird letters.

Variation: Play the game above. Then have each child choose one box and carefully arrange its letters on a sheet of paper before gluing them down. You might suggest that children make two or three lines of letters that cross each other horizontally, vertically, and/or diagonally on the paper. Alternatively, they might arrange a few letters to create real or nonsense words.

Explore a World of Letters

Materials: newspapers and magazines in foreign languages; safety scissors; paper; glue; crayons or markers

Collect publications in a variety of languages with different alphabets from the library, newspaper stands, and businesses (e.g., takeout menus). Show these to the group, pointing out how different they are. You can show texts in Russian, Arabic, Greek, Korean, Hindi—whatever you can find. Discuss with children the way people all over the world have invented different letters and characters to express their languages. If any bilingual children recognize their first language among the publications, invite them to tell about that alphabet and its sounds. (You may need to explain that some languages, such as Chinese, use characters that represent words or ideas instead of letters representing sounds.)

Allow children to explore the different alphabets. If some publications do not need to be returned, you could let children cut out their favorite letters and paste them onto paper.

Now invite children to make up their own letters and draw them. Children might design single letters to represent the sounds we spell using combinations of letters, such as *ch, th, sh,* and *oy.* Alternatively, they might design new letters to represent sounds that can't be expressed with our alphabet—for example: a whistle, a tongue cluck, a raspberry, a snap, or a clap. Then ask volunteers to show their imaginary letters to the group and "read" them aloud.

Morphing Letters

Materials: glue; paper; lowercase letters cut from construction paper—enough for each player to have several

Letters can be magically transformed. You can turn a *b* into a *p* by flipping it over. You can turn an *m* into an *n* by tearing one of the 'legs' off.

In advance, cut simple lowercase letters from construction paper. Be sure to include *b, d, p, q, o, h, j, m,* and *w;* you may wish to cut out other letters as well. Supply each child with several letters, and invite the children to transform the letters by rotating them, flipping them over, ripping parts of them off, or moving parts from one letter to another. Children can then paste the new letters they have created onto their piece of paper.

Note: If you color-code the letters (for example, make every *b* red), then it will be clear what letters the children started with.

Letter Pictures

Materials: paper; crayons or markers; letters from magazines; glue; safety scissors

Write the name of a familiar food or other object on the board. Invite children to create a picture of that object, including some of the letters in its name. For example, children might illustrate the word *soup* with a big capital *O* for the rim of the bowl, a big capital *U* for the bottom of the bowl, a lowercase *p* for the spoon, and a few lowercase *s*'s for the steam rising.

Depending on their proficiency, children can form their own letters or cut them out of old magazines and paste them onto paper. Tell children that their pictures don't need to be perfect, and it's not important to use every letter in the word. The point is to have fun with letter shapes.

Read My Lips

Materials: alphabet chart

Tell children that many deaf and hearing-impaired people learn to read lips—they can tell what a person is saying simply by watching her mouth move. Point out that your mouth moves quite differently when you say "eee" than it does when you say "buh." Display the alphabet and point to each letter as you make its sound, exaggerating the movements of your mouth. Then go through the alphabet again, but silently this time. Point to each letter as you mouth its sound. Now put the chart aside and invite children to read your lips as you silently mouth the sounds of various letters. If children recognize a letter, they should make its sound.

Variation: Children able to spell simple words might enjoy this variation. After playing the game above, divide the group into pairs. Have each pair think of a short word and spell it out for the group by mouthing it silently. Who can guess what the word is?

Note: Of course, many letters (the vowels and *y, c,* and *g*) make more than one sound in English. Choose the sound that you feel you can mouth most distinctly.

Letters in Action

Have players write down their names on scrap paper and think about what words begin with each letter of their names. Then challenge each player in turn to spell out his name for the rest of the group by miming words that begin with each letter. For example, a girl named Sue might mime the following words: *swimming, up, eating.*

It adds to the fun if the players have only just met. In this case, guessing becomes more of a challenge. This game is a fun way for players to learn each other's names.

Variation: Instead of miming, players can draw things that begin with the different letters of their names. (See the illustration below.) Collect the drawings, shuffle them, and hand them out. Challenge players to "read" the pictures and guess whose name they spell. The game becomes even more challenging if players create picture puzzles by scrambling the letters of their names before they make their drawings.

P=pear   A=ape   O=owl   L=lion   O=owl   = PAOLO

Sign Language

Materials: chart showing American Sign Language alphabet; video camera and player (optional)

In advance, search online or in an encyclopedia for a chart showing the alphabet in sign language. Practice making the signs for a few of the letters. To begin the game, tell the group that most deaf people learn to represent the alphabet with hand gestures. Display the chart, demonstrate some signs, and invite the group to try making the signs with you. Now divide the group into pairs and challenge them to invent their own hand gestures representing the letters of the alphabet. Will partners choose to portray the shape of each letter, or will they come up with a different way of portraying the letters? Tell partners that they need not cover all 26 letters. After 10 minutes, have each pair demonstrate one letter in its own sign language. Challenge the group to guess what letter each sign represents.

Variation: Have each pair invent signs for two or more assigned letters, making sure the entire alphabet is covered. Have pairs take turns showing their signs in alphabetical order, and make close-up video shots of the gestures. Then ask groups of two to four players to sign a short word in this new alphabet, using the video for reference if necessary. Challenge the other players to "read" each word.

Letter Scramble

In advance, choose several familiar words to scramble. Make sure the words are ones group members can spell easily. Still in advance, rearrange just one or two letters of each word and write that down. Write down two more arrangements for the letters in each word, each arrangement more scrambled than the last.

To begin the game, divide the group into teams of about four players each. On the board, write the most scrambled arrangement of letters for one of the words. Challenge team members to work together to unscramble the letters. If players are stuck, keep writing more recognizable arrangements of the letters on the board until one of the teams guesses the correct word. That team receives a point. If any team rearranges the letters to spell correctly a different word than the one you began with, they win a point too.

Note: This game can be adapted for younger children by using three- or four-letter words they can all recognize.

Newspaper Games

Newspapers are amazing things: Every day they offer a whole new parade of wonderful forms of language. The paper is full of words and expressions that you may or may not understand: place names from around the world, specialized lingo from business, science, and other fields, and neologisms—words newly coined to describe our changing world. On the page of a newspaper, completely unrelated things may be juxtaposed. You might find a sober news article right next to a comical advertisement. Newspapers are a rich source of material for all kinds of language games.

For this series of games you will need several pairs of scissors, large sheets of paper, glue, pens, storage boxes, and plenty of newspapers (both local and national). Make sure that you have everything ready in advance so that the games can begin and progress without delay.

The Same Word

Materials: newspapers; scissors; glue; sheets of paper

A word can appear in many different styles in a newspaper—there are hundreds of different typefaces. This game helps players discover how a very common word can suddenly look quite new.

Divide the group into pairs. Then ask each couple to find a simple word in the newspaper and cut out several different examples of the use of the same word. Have partners glue the words one below the other on a sheet of paper so that the different typefaces are clearly shown—capitals and lowercase letters, decorative and plain.

Display the sheets so that everyone can see them clearly. What moods do the various typefaces give each word? Can different styles make the same word seem stern, cheerful, sad, elegant, businesslike, or obnoxious?

today

TODAY

Today

today

today

The Singing Paper

Materials: newspapers; scissors; glue; sheets of paper

In every newspaper you can find examples of onomatopoeia—words suggesting a sound, such as *crash, boom, squeak, rap,* and so on. Have teams of about four players each search the newspaper for such words and clip them. Each team will then use its words to create a sound collage that can be sung. Just as in a piece of music, each sound can be repeated several times in the composition. (Players may find only one or two examples of a particular word. In that case, allow them to repeat the word by writing it in pen, but ask them not to write any new words they could not find in the paper.)

Give teams a few minutes to practice their compositions before performing them for the whole group. Encourage teams to enliven their performances with variations in pitch, tone, and volume.

Words Inside Words

Materials: newspapers; scissors; glue; sheets of paper; boxes (for variation)

Have players search the newspaper for very long words and clip them out. Encourage them to choose compound words. Now tell players that they will look for short words inside the long words they have found. Each player should glue the word that he thinks has the most possibilities onto a sheet of paper. Then the player can write down all the short words that long word contains. Tell players they only need to search for words that are spelled in sequence—they shouldn't try to recombine every single letter in the word. For example, *understandable* would yield *under, stand, able, tan, an, and,* and *dab.*

Once proficient players have found all the short words that can be spelled left-to-right, they might have fun looking for short words that can be spelled backward—this time, *understandable* would yield *bad, at,* and *red.* How many words can players find? Have them share their results with the group.

Variations:

- Have each player clip four or five long words and write them on a piece of paper. Then players should cut each long word into shorter words with scissors and scramble the pieces in a small box. Invite players to trade boxes and lists of short words that were found in long words and try to reassemble the long words from the short words in the box.

- Ask all the players to clip long words from the newspaper, cut them into parts, and pile the pieces where everyone can reach them. Then invite everyone to combine various word parts to create nonsense words. Players can paste their nonsense words onto sheets of paper. Have players display them and read them aloud. Which words are the silliest? Are there any words that actually mean something?

- After playing the variation above, have each player choose a couple of nonsense words, think up meanings for them, and introduce the new words to the group.

- As a variation on the assignment above, ask each player to pass her best or silliest word to her neighbor, who then must think up three possible meanings for the word. Which meaning sounds the most probable?

Clipping the Headlines

Materials: newspapers; scissors; glue; sheets of paper

Have each player clip four or five headlines from newspapers. Then ask players to cut each headline into a few pieces—a piece might contain a few words, a single word, or just part of a word.

Invite players to rearrange these pieces to create new, unexpected headlines. Tell players they can swap headline pieces with their neighbors if they wish. Challenge players to create the most humorous, interesting, or thrilling headline. Players can paste their new headlines onto sheets of paper and display them to the rest of the group.

Headline
Scramble

Materials: newspapers; scissors; glue; sheets of paper

Have each player clip one newspaper headline and then cut it in half. Then have players sit in a circle and have each player place half a headline into the center. Players should shuffle the pile of headline halves. At your signal, each player should pass her remaining headline half to the player on her right. Players must search the pile for the words that come before or after the headline half that was passed to them. As players complete their headlines, they can help their neighbors.

Variation: After playing the game above, reshuffle the headline halves and have players recombine them to create new headlines. Challenge players to create new complete sentences. Are any of the new headlines improvements on the old ones?

Headline Puzzles

Materials: newspapers; scissors; glue; sheets of paper

Have pairs of players create headline puzzles for each other. Each player should clip one newspaper headline. Encourage players to choose long headlines. Players should then cut the headline into five or six pieces (each containing one or more complete words) and glue about half the pieces onto a sheet of paper in the position they had in the original headline. The gaps remain open. Have partners trade puzzles and try to fit the missing pieces into each headline.

Variation: This time, have players create puzzles with missing letters instead of missing words. Encourage players to make sure part of each word remains recognizable. Players try to solve each other's puzzles by completing the words. They can also change or improve the words. What new headlines will be created?

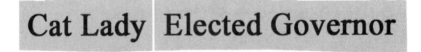

Cat Lady Elected Governor

Ad-lib Ads

Materials: photos without text clipped from newspapers and magazines; newspapers; scissors; glue; sheets of paper

In advance, clip some interesting photos from newspapers and magazines, making sure not to include any text. Put the photos out in a pile where everyone can reach them.

Point out to players that the newspapers are filled with advertisements that use the most fantastic sentences to praise a product. Have players search newspapers for dramatic slogans and other advertising copy. Players should clip the slogans they find and gather them in a pile next to the photos. Then have players look through the materials and select a photo and one or more slogans. Players should combine the photo and the ad copy on a sheet of paper, pasting them together to form a new and unexpected advertisement. Then have players display and discuss their creations.

Photo
Finish

Materials: plenty of newspaper photos; newspapers; scissors; glue; sheets of paper

In advance, choose a few striking newspaper photographs to show players. Point out that newspaper photos can be informative, shocking, disturbing, or comical. Display the photos, read the captions, and discuss the feelings they evoke.

   Then have players search through newspapers for photos to cut out. Each player should glue her photo to a sheet of paper. Underneath she should write a new caption, a short made-up news report, or some dialog. The text can explain something about the photograph or it could be something totally unexpected. When players are finished, have them show their work to the rest of the group and discuss it.

20

Good News or Bad News?

Materials: short newspaper articles

In advance, clip several short newspaper articles and, if possible, use a photocopier to enlarge them. Choose articles on a variety of subjects, from articles on election results to film reviews to articles on sports events. Display the articles and point out that everyone has a different way of reading the news. A member of the winning team might read an article about a basketball game gleefully. The same article might be read morosely by a fan of the losing team or defensively by a player on that team. Demonstrate by reading a short section of one article straightforwardly, and then from a few different perspectives.

Now have each team choose an article and think of different ways to read it aloud. Different team members might play the following roles: a movie reviewer, an actor criticized in a review, a politician who has lost an election, the winner of the election, and so on. Readers should show with their tone of voice their perspective and how they feel about the story. When teams have practiced for 15 minutes or so, ask them to take turns reading aloud brief excerpts to the whole group. Invite the group to guess what role each reader is playing.

21

What Happened Next?

Materials: newspaper articles and headlines; scissors; glue; sheets of paper; a folder

In advance, clip several stories with intriguing headlines. Cut the headlines out and save the stories in a folder. Divide the group into teams of about four players each. Have each team choose a headline and paste it at the top of a sheet of paper. Then the team members should work together to write the first sentence of a story that might follow the headline. These sentences are passed on to another group who adds another sentence and passes the paper on again. Teams should continue passing papers around and adding sentences to them until every group has contributed to every story and the stories are several sentences long. Have each team read aloud the news report they began. Then read aloud a few sentences of the actual newspaper story that ran under that headline. Invite players to discuss how the made-up stories differ from the genuine articles.

How Does It End?

Materials: newspaper articles; newspapers: scissors; glue; sheets of paper

Read a couple of short newspaper articles to the group. About half-way through each one, stop and ask the group: How does it end? Invite volunteers to make guesses before you read the rest of the story aloud. Then divide the group into teams of about four players.

Each team should find and clip a short but interesting newspaper article of not more than 20 lines. Ask team members to decide on an intriguing point about halfway through the story and cut the article in two at that point. They should paste the top half of the story onto a sheet of paper and swap papers with another team. Then team members work together to come up with an ending to the new story they have been given and write it on the sheet of paper. Have groups take turns reading their newly created endings. Then ask the group that chose each story to read out the original text. Is the new text very different from the original?

A Newspaper Story

Materials: newspapers; scissors; glue; sheets of paper

Ask the group to clip out a large number of headlines and gather them all together. Then divide the group into teams of about four players each and distribute an equal number of headlines to each team. Invite each team to work together to arrange its headlines so that they tell a kind of story. Then teams should glue the headlines onto a sheet of paper in the appropriate order. Can each team manage with the texts they have? Encourage teams to use only lines from the newspaper to tell their stories, but allow teams that are really stuck to write a few short words between the headlines.

Variation: You might try asking each team to clip out the following: four names, four jobs, four places, and four times. Then each team should devise a story from these. In this variation, teams will, of course, need to add their own verbs, adjectives, and so on to flesh out the story.

Sensory Games

We are constantly using our senses as we communicate. We use our sense of sight to read words, of course, but we also use it to watch a person's gestures and expressions as she speaks, to notice different styles and colors of letters, and to form mental images of the words we read or hear. We use our sense of hearing to listen to the words a person says, but also to notice his tone of voice, how he pronounces words, and where he places emphasis.

Although we may be less aware of it, language also involves the use of our other senses. Different words call to mind flavors, smells, and textures. You can almost taste the words on a good menu. People with impaired vision actually read by touch, using the Braille alphabet.

These games help players train their senses and become more aware of what they want to watch for, listen to, and observe as they use language.

Seeing Words

Materials: drawing paper; crayons or markers

Point out to players that the words we read or hear can create pictures in our minds. Some words, such as *truck*, create specific pictures, while others, such as *cozy*, might create different mental pictures for everyone. Pass out paper and have players fold their sheets in half twice, to create four sections. Four times, say a word aloud and have players spend a couple of minutes sketching the picture it creates in their minds. For young children, you might begin with a concrete noun, such as *dinosaur*. Move on to adjectives such as *soft, fierce, glamorous,* or *bleak*—these words may inspire more varied and interesting drawings. Invite players to display their drawings to the group and discuss what they drew and why.

Variations:

- You might adapt the game for older players by having them describe in writing the mental images selected words produce.

- Read aloud a haiku or other very short poem and have players draw the mental images it inspires.

Hearing Words

This is an auditory version of game 11 (Letter Scramble). In advance, choose several familiar, short words to scramble. Make sure the words are ones group members can spell easily. Still in advance, rearrange just one or two letters of each word and write that scrambled-letter word down. Write down two more arrangements for the letters in each word, each arrangement more scrambled than the last.

Tell players you will read out scrambled letters, and they should try to guess what word the letters could spell. Begin with the most scrambled arrangement of letters for each word. If players have trouble guessing, read other arrangements that come closer and closer to the correct spelling of the word. Be sure to begin with very easy words, and help players along by keeping a key combination together in each word, such as the *ppl* in *apple*. Once players get the hang of the game, make it more challenging.

Feeling Words

Materials: cardboard; pipe cleaners; tape; alphabet refrigerator magnets; a Braille book from the library (optional)

Point out to the group that people who can't see often learn to read by touch. If possible, display a book in Braille and explain that each group of raised bumps represents a different letter. Invite players to try recognizing letters by touch. Have players close their eyes and hand them letter-shaped refrigerator magnets to feel and identify.

Tell players they can create their own touchable letters and words. Have them bend pipe cleaners into letter shapes and tape them onto cardboard. Players can then close their eyes, trade creations, and identify the letters or words.

Feeling letters sounds easy, but players' motor and visual memories have to work hard!

Eat Your Words

Materials: flat foods such as sliced bread, tortillas, or baked filo dough; squeeze bottles of honey or catsup; napkins or paper plates

Which words are the most delicious? Invite players to list words that make them hungry, from names of favorite foods to yummy adjectives to words that just sound like they would taste good.

Have players pick the best word from their list. Then provide players with slices of bread (or another flat food) and let them write their words in honey (or another squeezable food). Players can read their words aloud and then eat them. These are words that players can see, hear, touch, smell, and taste.

Let the Mood Move You

Point out to the group that sometimes the words people say are not as important as *how* we say them. To demonstrate, say "I'm fine" three times: first quickly and cheerfully, next slowly and sadly, and finally loudly and angrily. Invite volunteers to tell what message they would receive from each statement. Tell players that the object of this game is to pay attention to the way a person is speaking.

Have players spread out around the room. Explain that you are going to repeat a single word—you might choose a simple command like "move," or you might choose an amusing word like "pumpernickel." Outline for players a few tone-of-voice signals that will tell them how to move. For example, saying the word sadly means they should walk very slowly; a high voice means players should stand on tiptoe; a whisper means they should crouch down; and so on. Play the game for a few minutes with open eyes. Then have players line up side-by-side at one end of the room, spread out as far apart as they can, and move to your signals with their eyes closed. Keep a close eye on players in order to prevent collisions. Warn players that everyone should stop moving if you call "stop!"

Variation: Add to the challenge by constantly changing the word you say. Remind players not to pay attention to *what* you say; it's *how* you say it that is important.

I Hear the Waves Crashing

Materials: cassette or CD player; homemade or commercially produced recordings of environmental sounds or other sound effects

In advance, make or find a set of sound recordings. At the library you may be able to find New Age albums of environmental sounds such as waves and bird songs. Any wordless, nonmusical sounds will do.

Have players write down the sounds they hear. Players might begin by writing guesses as to what made the sound. Encourage them to go beyond this to describe the sound using adjectives and, perhaps, to write about the images or feelings the sounds evoke.

Variation: You could adapt this game to exercise players' sense of smell. Have players close their eyes and hold out fragrant objects for players to sniff: coffee, laundry detergent, orange slices, soap, bread, pine sprigs, and so on. Keep the objects hidden so that players experience them only through smell. Players can open their eyes and write a few words or phrases describing and attempting to identify each scent.

The **Sound**
of **Words**

In advance, write out a list of words that you feel have interesting sounds. Try to avoid onomatopoeia—words that are specifically intended to evoke certain sounds, such as *bang* or *drip*.

Invite the group to think about how words really sound. There are elegant-sounding words, such as *camouflage*; ugly-sounding words, such as *blurb*; and silly-sounding words, such as *snorkel*. Do some words have sounds that don't match their meanings? Does the word *pretty* really sound all that pretty? Invite players to brainstorm words that sound silly or elegant to them. Then begin reading words from your list. For each word, have players write an adjective or two describing how that word sounds to them. Encourage players to concentrate on the sounds of the words, rather than their meanings. Next to "xylophone" one player might write "bright," while another might write "splashy." When players are done, read your list again and have volunteers share their impressions of each word. The same word can sound very different to different people!

Introduction Games

As children play together, they get to know each other. Language is a wonderful medium for this. Players speak or write to each other, tell each other all sorts of things, and thus learn more and more about each other. Language games help players learn how others react to them and how others express themselves.

This kind of exchange is only possible in a supportive atmosphere. Players must feel secure and free enough to express themselves openly. Introduction games help build such an atmosphere. These games are designed to be noncompetitive and nonconfrontational. As leader, you can help create an open atmosphere by changing pairings often, keeping games short, making frequent positive comments, and refraining from unnecessary criticism of players' performance.

When I Grow Up...

Invite everyone to sit in a circle. Ask players whether they have any ideas about what they would like to do or be when they grow up. Do they want jobs that involve excitement? Do they want to help others? Do they want to use talents such as singing, writing, or playing soccer? Go around the circle and invite players to share their ambitions. Encourage players to choose jobs or other basically realistic dreams for this round. You could join in by revealing an ambition you hope to fulfil someday (visiting Teotihuacán, writing a novel, whatever comes to mind). Alternatively, you could inspire players with a story about a personal childhood ambition that you fulfilled.

Now invite players to imagine they could be anything at all—a fantasy creature, a dinosaur, a character from a book or movie, or any other fantastical identity. Go around the circle again and let players share their wildest dreams.

Variations:

- Change the focus of the game from *what* do you want to be to *who* do you want to be. Many children aren't as interested in a particular job as they are in following in the footsteps of their greatest idol. Ask each member of the group in turn who their heroes are and why.

- Have older players write down what they want to do or who they want to be without signing the paper. Then read aloud each ambition and ask the group members to guess who wrote it. It makes a very good guessing game, particularly when the players don't yet know each other very well. If no one can guess the player's identity, ask him to reveal himself.

Group Cheer

Tell the group that they need to work together as a team. Point out that cheerleaders use cheers to support their team. Give them an example of a well-known cheer, such as: "2-4-6-8! Who do we appreciate? Team! Team! Go, team!" Tell players that cheers should be short and rhythmic, so they can be shouted easily. A cheer might rhyme, but it does not have to. A cheer may work towards a climax—for instance: "We are good; we are better; we're the best!"

Divide the group into teams of about four players. Invite each team to work together to create a cheer for the whole group. Have them practice their cheers for about 10 minutes. Then invite each team to present its cheer to the group. After hearing each cheer once or twice, the group can repeat it all together.

Yea!!!!

Variation: Agree on a signal that means everyone should be silent and another signal that means everyone should cheer. Have all the teams rehearse their cheers at full volume. Give the signal for silence, then ask one group to continue cheering alone. Give the signal for everyone to cheer again, and repeat the exercise until each team has had a chance to cheer alone. Keep up a brisk pace so that teams don't feel singled out: Each team's turn should last for only one or two repetitions of its cheer.

Matchmaker

Materials: notecards

Pass out a blank notecard to each player. Ask players to write a word that describes them on the card—*goalie, brave, singer, giggler*, or any word that fits. Then tell players that they should try to find another player with a card that fits with theirs. It's unlikely that they will find an exact match; they should just look for a pair of words with something in common.

When two cards fit together, the players should raise their hands and explain how their words are similar. They can keep trying to find new combinations, until everyone has matched her card at least once. If players are stuck, help them discover unexpected links between words: A *goalie* has to be *brave*, and so on.

Note: This game works only with people who do not yet know each other. You will get all sorts of strange combinations!

Do You Like Liver?

Divide the group into pairs who sit facing each other. Have one player in each pair write the headings _Fun_ and _Delicious_ on a sheet of paper, and beneath each heading write a word the player associates with it. The player passes the sheet to his partner, who reacts with two words of her own. Have partners take turns adding words for a few minutes.

Now have one partner turn the sheet over and write the headings _No Fun_ and _Bad Tasting_. Partners can have fun passing the sheet back and forth and sharing their dislikes.

Q&A

Write a number of get-acquainted questions on the board, such as: *What is your name? What place do you dream of visiting someday? What's your favorite food/music/hobby/sport/book/television show?* Divide the group into pairs and have one partner interview the other. After a few minutes let players switch roles. After a few minutes more change partners so that each member of the group can get to know several other people.

Invite players to share the most interesting facts they learned about one another.

Note: Avoid questions that stray onto the too-personal ground of home life or ones that reveal players' financial situations, such as *What is your house like? What kind of car does your family have?*

36

pairs

Nice to Meet You

You can learn a lot about how people feel and think from the way they choose their words.

Divide the group into pairs who sit facing each other. Have one player from each pair write the word *meet* at the top of a sheet of paper and pass it to her partner. The partner writes down a word that *meet* suggests to him. The pair passes the paper back and forth, reading each other's words, making associations, and adding new words. After a few minutes have players switch partners. The new pairs turn their sheets over and use *meet* to begin a new series of word associations.

Variation: In the second round, players can write their lists next to the last one so that the differences are immediately apparent.

My Favorite Word

Point out to the group that we all have favorite words we like to use: *whatever, amazing, paradigm*. Certain words have a special ring to each person. Everyone feels differently: A word that delights one person may mean nothing to someone else.

Ask each player to make a list of ten words that sound special to him. Then invite volunteers to share some or all of their words with the group. Have players discuss what it is they like about the words they chose.

whatever

Variation: Ask players to think of words that irritate them as well as words they like. Have them rank their lists, with their favorite word at the top and the worst word at the bottom.

We the Players...

This game is designed to encourage an atmosphere of mutual respect in a writing or storytelling class. Point out that the members of a new group have all kinds of unexpressed expectations. Group members expect to feel comfortable, learn new skills, gain understanding, have fun with the others, and so on. Explain that in this class, group members will be expressing themselves through writing or telling stories. It is important that all the members of the group respect each other as they work together on, listen to, or comment on projects.

Invite group members to brainstorm guidelines for how they would like to be treated in class. Do they want quiet as they tell a story? Do they want teams to make decisions about projects unanimously, or by majority vote? Depending on the group's level of experience, you may need to make suggestions and explain what sort of activities they will be doing in the class. Have volunteers take notes on the board. Then ask the group to work together to compile a short list of informal group rules. They might write it as a group constitution. The group should make sure all members are satisfied with the results. Then everyone can sign the paper. As the class goes on and the members gain more experience, the group may decide to change, discard, or add rules.

39

Biography

Materials: baby pictures of each player

Most of us are almost unrecognizable in our baby pictures. In advance, ask players to bring in (replaceable) photos of themselves as babies or toddlers. Have players work in pairs: a narrator and a biographer. The narrator displays her baby pictures and recounts a few memorable childhood anecdotes. The biographer takes notes and then writes a story about the narrator. He should avoid using any real names and can use his imagination to embellish the story. Then the partners should switch roles and repeat the exercise.

Display the stories on a bulletin board with the appropriate baby pictures taped to them. Can the rest of the group guess who each story is about?

Sound Games

Silence has become rare. Many people hardly know what silence is any more. We wake up to an alarm clock, the microwave dings to tell us food is ready, computers squawk to tell us we have e-mail, and cell phones beep their cheery songs everywhere we go.

There are all kinds of sounds in the world: mechanical noises, the roar of engines, animal sounds, the atmospheric sounds of nature, and so on. The human voice is frequently brilliant at imitating these inhuman sounds. Think, for instance, of rappers who conjure with sounds as well as with words.

In these games, players explore the boundaries and interrelationships between sound and language. There are breathing and vocalization exercises that help warm up the voice for public speaking and storytelling. There are sound effect games in which players think about, identify, describe, and recreate sounds. These games help players discover how language becomes sound and sound becomes language.

Exhaling

We all breathe without thinking, but most of us don't use our lungs efficiently. Many people don't exhale completely: Part of the breath just gets left behind.

Have players sit in a wide circle, arms loose by their sides. Demonstrate breathing in and out deeply. Breathe in through the nose and out through the mouth. Let players practice breathing deeply for a minute or so. Now add sound. Begin with a simple "ah" sound on each exhalation, and have players chant along. Then go through the long vowel sounds:

$$/ \bar{a} /, / \bar{e} /, / \bar{i} /, / \bar{o} /, / \bar{u} /$$

Encourage players to let the sound of each vowel carry as long as they can, until their lungs are completely empty. Then have them make all the vowel sounds in one breath.

Do this as a group and then let players practice independently. This game is a good warm-up for using the voice.

Note: Deep breathing always carries the risk of hyperventilation. Ask players to stop and breathe normally if they feel light-headed or faint.

41

The Same Sound

Tell players that you will make a sound, and they should copy it. Take a deep breath and vocalize a stretched-out nonsense combination of vowel sounds and consonants, such as *chaaaoooeeeehh-mmmm*. Make a few more sounds for the group to copy. Now have players take the initiative. Each player in turn makes a stretched-out sound that is repeated by the rest of the group.

This game is a good warm-up for using the voice. It helps players feel free to improvise and let their voices be heard—important activities in storytelling.

Variations:

- Some young children find it hard to make sounds on demand like this. You may want to adapt the game by combining it with a fairy tale. This way the sounds also acquire an emotional charge: Children will have little problem in imitating the sound of a fierce wolf, a sneaky witch, or a slow, sad snail. Once players have the hang of the game, you might stop the story whenever a new animal or character is introduced. Ask the group what kind of sound the animal or character might make. Let a volunteer make a suggestion and have the others join in.

- Each player makes his own series of sounds and keeps repeating it. They walk around the room making the kinds of movements they think the animal or thing they are portraying in sound might make. Whenever players meet, they demonstrate their sounds to each other. Do the sounds clash, or do they complement each other? Encourage players to find sounds that fit with their own and to form pairs or small groups, thereby creating longer sound patterns. When players have combined, invite each pair or group to perform their sounds for everyone.

Voice Tricks

Materials: cardboard tubes, tissue paper, large cardboard boxes, traffic cones, and other objects players can use to muffle or amplify their voices

Point out to children that their voices sound different on the playground than they do in a small room. Then demonstrate a few other ways in which an object influences the voice: Talk through a sheet of tissue paper, use your hands as a megaphone, or put your head in a cardboard box and talk through it. Now invite children to discover how they can change their voices using the objects you have provided.

After a few minutes of exploring, invite children to share the tricks they can perform with their own voices.

What Sound Does a Fridge Make?

Seat children on the floor in a circle and join them. Make a few animal and household noises and invite children to identify each sound and then copy it. Now ask the group: What sound does a mouse make? What sound does a telephone make? What sound does a wolf make? What sound does a fridge make?

Finally, invite players to name sounds of their own and challenge the group to make them. If the other players cannot think of a way to reproduce a particular sound, the player who suggested it makes it himself. Then the rest can copy him.

A Story with Sound Effects

Read or tell a story that includes a selection of sounds. Stop periodically and ask how the pig grunted, how the bell rang, how the footsteps sounded on the stones, and so on. The players can make all the sounds as a group, but it works better if you call on one volunteer to make each sound. In the beginning this may slow the story down, but the timing will improve as the group warms up.

In a group with very young children, it is fun to read the same story again the next day. Small children love to repeat the sounds they have learned.

If Animals Could Talk

Ask children: What noises do cats make when they are happy? What noises do angry dogs make? Point out that animals don't use words the way we do, but they can communicate some simple messages, such as "Feed me!" and "Go away!"

Invite children to imagine that animals could talk in their own language. Would a horse neigh its words? What might a talking cow sound like?

Divide the group into pairs. Have partners choose what animals they would like to be. Partners could be the same species, or different ones. Invite each pair to carry on a conversation in "animalese." Farm animals might talk about life on the farm, forest animals might talk about hunters or the coming winter, and so on.

A Noise in the Dark

We all hear strange sounds at night, sounds we can't identify. Divide the group into fours. Each team thinks up, discusses, and rehearses a scary or weird noise that they can make for the group. Have the group close their eyes as each team performs its noise. Then the group should try to identify the sound. If no one can guess correctly, the team should explain what the sound is supposed to be.

You can add to the atmosphere by dimming the lights or lighting the room with candles. You might also ask the groups to describe their sounds on paper. Is there perhaps a story behind the sound that could provide an idea for a script?

Not a Bangbangbang, a Zzzzt-zzzzzt

Divide the group into teams of about four. Have players imagine they are visiting a country where the names of most things are based on the sounds they make. For example, the word for "snake" might be *sssss*, and the word for "water" might be *splashdrip*.

Have teams invent several sound-words and use them in a skit they act out for the group. Teams might enact silly scenes in a pet store or tool shop: "Do you want to buy a bangbangbang?" "No, I need a zzzzt-zzzzzt!" "Oh, a plinkplink?" After 10 minutes of practice the teams perform their skits for the group.

Sound Boxes

Materials: three or four large cardboard boxes; rhythm instruments or other objects for making sounds

In advance, gather large cardboard boxes; some players may be able to bring boxes from home. Each box should be big enough for two children to sit inside and still have some wiggle room. Explain that players will make these into giant sound boxes (like music boxes): Inside they will create a world of their own with a few objects and sounds. Make a flap in the box so that the other players can put their ears to the hole to listen.

Divide the group into pairs. Ask each pair to think up an environment in which sounds and objects have a role to play. They can either go ahead and create a sound box that stands alone or they can attempt to make a sound box that connects to a story. Let pairs rehearse for 15 minutes. Different pairs can take turns trying out their sounds inside the boxes. When the pairs are ready, they can begin giving their performances. Choose one pair to start out in each box. Have the pairs in the boxes make their noises and invite the rest of the group to walk around listening at the holes. After a few minutes, let new pairs perform in the boxes.

Variation: If several rooms are available to you, set up a different box in each one. The game is even more fun when the listeners don't know who is in each box.

Consonants
and Vowels

Materials: letters from a game such as Scrabble™ or letters cut from magazine titles or newspaper headlines; a bag or box for holding letters

Have each player pick seven letters out of a bag and arrange them in the order in which they were chosen. Then invite players to pronounce their new "words." There may be several consonants or vowels in a row: *kptazmi, euuqmlb,* and so on. This adds to the fun. Encourage players to invent funny sounds suggested by these random letter combinations.

Now pour the letters out into a pile and invite players to choose whatever letters they want and arrange them into funny nonsense combinations. Have players take turns saying their invented words aloud to the group. Then have players make up meanings for the words.

Write the invented words and meanings on the board. Have players pair up and try using some of the words in a silly conversation.

Sounds of the Body

Materials: cassette recorder with microphone and blank tape (optional)

Point out that words are not the only noises we can make. The human body can make a huge number of sounds: People can laugh, sniff, stamp their feet, cluck their tongues, and so on. Divide the group into fours and have each team choose a situation or location where people gather—for example: a restaurant, a football game or other sports event, a sleeping coach on the train, or a line of people waiting to see a movie. Have each team work together to create a sound portrait of that situation. Teams should not use props in their portraits; they should use only sounds made by the body. Ask team members to think of many different sounds that fit their situation and to spread those sounds out over a minute or so. Encourage them to build the scene over the whole minute, building up to a climax.

Let teams practice for 10 minutes and then perform for the whole group. You may wish to tape the various performances and play them back. You will notice that just listening has a completely different effect from listening and watching at the same time.

Note: Inevitably, this game invites mischievous noises—belching, passing wind, and so on. If you are playing in a context where such noises are unacceptable, or if you feel a particular group will get completely out of hand, you may want to choose another game.

The
Ventriloquist

Materials: hand puppets with moveable mouths

Ask players to tell what they know about ventriloquists. If necessary, explain that a ventriloquist is a performer who does a comedy act with a dummy—a kind of puppet. The ventriloquist provides the dummy's voice, but keeps her own mouth closed. A good ventriloquist creates the illusion that the dummy is talking and she is silent. Ventriloquists practice long and hard to learn to speak without moving their mouths. Certain sounds are easy, but others are nearly impossible.

Divide the group into pairs and give each pair a hand puppet or two. Have partners take turns trying to talk without moving their mouths. Encourage them to explore making all kinds of sounds, both vowels and consonants. Partners should watch each other to see which sounds work best. Then invite them to think up a few sentences that include their best sounds. Partners can now practice ventriloquism, using the hand puppets as dummies and saying their lines without moving their mouths. Tell players not to become discouraged: Ventriloquism is a highly specialized and difficult art. This game is not concerned with perfection; it is simply a way to explore spoken language. After 10 or 15 minutes, let volunteers perform for the group. Discuss which sounds are hardest to make without moving the mouth, and why this might be.

Symphony of Screams

Except on roller coasters, at sports games, or at horror movies, the scream is a voice we rarely have the chance to use. In this game, players can let themselves go, not haphazardly, but loudly and clearly. In advance, find a spot where players can shout and yell without disturbing anyone: perhaps an athletic field or a sound-proofed music practice room.

Give an introductory talk about the different ways in which people all over the world express their joys and sorrows. Warn players that in order to spare the vocal cords it is best not to begin by screaming at full volume, but to build from soft to loud on a long, slow exhalation. You might have players rehearse this as you conduct the ebb and flow of the sounds. Now divide the group into teams of about six or eight. Each team decides which sound they are going to make. Will it be a cry of misery or a cheer of victory? If you are in a large outdoor area, have each team choose a spot removed from the others but still within hearing distance. Now have them practice on location. Move from group to group, listening to the sounds. Finally, ask each group to make its sound in turn, as the others listen from a short distance away. Discuss how it feels to scream, and what the screams sounded like.

Mystery Sounds

There are countless sounds to be heard in and around the house. In advance, ask players to write down all the interesting sounds they hear for a week. Players should not only name the sound ("a computer humming"), they should also try to write it in letters ("himmna himmna").

himmna himmna

Have players choose their favorite sound—the one they think they captured most accurately, the most unusual sound they heard, or the one that surprised them most with its beauty. Invite players to take turns writing their sound on the board, imitating it, and challenging the group to identify it. If no one can guess the source of the sound correctly, have players give hints about where the sound can be heard, how the sound is made or used, and so on.

What Sounds Do You See?

Materials: some images that evoke sounds (many-featured land-scapes or city scenes, for example)

Some images are so expressive, so eloquent, that you can almost hear the sounds they evoke. Bring some examples (photographs, drawings, or slides) to show to the group. Choose an image and tell players what sounds it conjures up for you. For example, tell players what you can hear in the thickly branched tree, what you think the waters of that beautiful lake would sound like, or what the smoke from that airplane tells you about its sound. What is hiding behind an animal or object in a drawing or photo? By asking such questions, you will stimulate the group's creativity. Now divide the group into teams of four to six players. Each team chooses a picture, discusses it, and practices the sounds it suggests to them. After 15 or 20 minutes of practice, each team performs its piece in front of the group. If time allows, invite discussion about each sound performance. You might ask players to point out the places in a picture where they see the sounds.

Variations:

- In advance, ask each player to bring in a favorite photo or an illustration from a book. Teams can use these as the basis of their sound performances.

- Abstract pictures can also be "translated" into sound. Working together with a drawing or painting class could result in an exhibition of images and sounds.

Sound and Fury Signifying Something

Point out that people often communicate without words. Sounds play a very important role in the expression of emotions. In an emergency situation, people may make wordless sounds that are clearly understandable: for example, a scream of terror, a warning shout, or a groan of pain. Tell players they are going to explore this special language.

Divide the group into teams of four or so. Have each group work together to create a performance piece: one minute of sounds in an emergency situation. Allow players to include a few words and sentences if necessary, but encourage them to make inarticulate sounds the focus of the performance. While the teams are practicing, give them advice and ideas. After 15 or 20 minutes, invite teams to perform their pieces for the rest of the group. Then let players discuss their experiences making and listening to these sounds.

Note: For some groups, this game could release strong emotions, so include enough time for debriefing. It is good to let children imagine such situations, as it will help them to get more of a grip on their fears.

Storytelling Games

Storytelling is an ancient art form that is still very much alive. People all over the world treasure this mode of communication: It is a means of passing on not just old stories, but also the shared values and customs that make up a culture.

For storytelling, you don't need a pen, nor do you need to waste paper. The story originates in the heart and the head, takes form in spoken words, and grows in the telling. Adventure stories, whether true or fictional, have always had tremendous appeal. Think of the tales of heroes the ancients told on long winter evenings—a wonderful substitute for today's television!

Anyone can learn the art of storytelling. You can learn to listen attentively, tune your voice, and choose your words carefully. You can tell a story you already know or, of course, you can make one up. The greatest challenge of storytelling is constructing a plot that will come across well, but even this can be learned with practice. The section About Composing Stories on page 6 will help you guide a beginning group through the steps of constructing a compelling story. The games in this section will give players the opportunity to hone their storytelling skills.

Good Morning

Have the group sit in a circle with you. Spend a few minutes telling the group about how you got up this morning and prepared for the day. Include sensory details and any interesting or unusual events. Talk about the pleasant and less pleasant sides and include both busy times and periods of calm in the story. Tension and relaxation alternate with each other.

Now have players go around the circle and tell their own morning stories. There are no limitations; everyone simply gives a short account of their experiences.

Variations:

- Have players describe the events of last evening instead of this morning. How do they get ready for bed? What do their rooms look like in the dark?

- Ask players to avoid repeating the same phrases and sentences others have used in telling their stories. Players will have to think about their stories carefully. How many ways can they think of to describe getting out of bed? What made their mornings different from everyone else's?

- With a group of older children, you might try telling about your morning in impressionistic phrases, emphasizing the feelings and the senses, rather than stating the morning's events. Bring to life all the things one sees and does in the mornings. Thus, the stories can become improvised spoken-word poems.

Where
I Live

Materials: photographs (optional)

This game uses as its starting point the place where the players live and the way they came to the class. This game is very suitable for groups that have little experience with storytelling and do not yet know each other very well.

Have the group sit in a circle. Go around the circle and invite each player to tell a story about where she lives and how she arrived at the school (or the place where the class is being held). Each player may choose whether her story will be fiction or nonfiction: A player might describe her own home, a house from a favorite story, or a made-up house. She might tell about her actual trip to the class or about an imaginary journey. If a player needs prompting, ask questions during the story or after it has ended. (Be sure that players are not pressured to tell about their real homes or home life: Players should always have the option of telling fictional stories.)

Variations:

- Encourage all the players to describe their homes as far more beautiful than they really are and give a lyrical, poetic description of their journey to the class.

- Let players illustrate their stories with beautiful photographs that have absolutely nothing to do with where they really live.

A **Story Full** of **Holes**

A few days before playing this game, tell the children a story. You could read a storybook to them or tell them an original story.

To begin the game, have players sit in a circle. Explain that you will read or tell the same story you did before, but this time you want their help in telling it. As you read or tell the story, stop periodically in the middle of a memorable event. ("He huffed and he....") Invite players to jump in and fill the "hole" in the story. Then continue until you come to the next hole. The members of the group have to stay alert so they can jump in as soon as there is a hole in the story.

The **Theater** of **Storytelling**

Materials: cloth; paper; art materials; and masking tape

This is a special game designed for the end of a semester of classes or a similar occasion. The group will need to spend a couple of hours (which could be broken up over the course of a week) to prepare in advance for the final presentation.

Divide the group into teams of about four players. You might have each team make up its own story, or you might choose one long story and assign part of it to each team. Team members should work together on how to present their story. Then have each team choose a space in which to tell its story. Depending on the spaces available to you, players might choose a piece of playground equipment, the space under stadium bleachers, or simply a classroom corner. Encourage teams to try to find a space that suits the mood of the story they are telling. Have teams practice telling their stories in their spaces.

Plan a time for the final storytelling presentation and invite an audience—players' friends and families or perhaps another class. In advance, teams should prepare decorations for their spaces with paper and art materials. Just before the presentation, tape up the decorations and drape the spaces with cloth to transform them into dimly lit stages. Have the teams gather in their spaces. Invite the audience to tour all the spaces—in chronological order, if teams are telling parts of a single story. Depending on the size of the audience, you may want to break it up into small groups. When listeners arrive at their space, each team should be ready to present their story.

Note: If lighting and regulations allow, hold the final presentation in the evening rather than during the day. This adds to the atmosphere of excitement.

ᴀ **Collection of Figments**

Every child collects something, whether it be model horses, cars, or dinosaurs; books by a favorite author; or fossils, shells, and other natural objects. Perhaps in the end, the act of collecting is more important than the objects themselves. Everyone is fascinated by strange collections and the stories behind them. Invite players to describe (briefly) any collections they have created.

Divide the group into teams of about four players. Invite the teams to imagine a category of make-believe objects and give these a name: singing stones, tickle machines, snorkel snails, whatever comes to mind. Ask players: What are the objects like? What can they be used for? What are your favorite objects in the collection? Where did you collect these objects? Teams can describe the place where they started their collection, the journeys there and back, and the discovery itself. After the teams have had time to work out the details, ask each team to tell the group about its imaginary collection.

Comic Relief

Materials: children's joke books

Telling a joke seems simple, but it's not as easy as it sounds. Many people give away the punch line before they've told the joke or don't know how to build up the tension. This game uses jokes to help players develop their storytelling abilities.

Tell the players a joke or two to get them started. Then divide the group into pairs. Invite players to pick jokes out of a joke book or recall ones they have heard before. Partners should take turns telling their jokes to each other. They can try out different approaches and give each other feedback. It is great fun to help each other to tell a joke well. Listen in on partners practicing and give encouragement as well as suggestions on timing, building tension, and delivering the punch line. Then have players present their jokes to the group. It might be fun to invite people from outside the group to enjoy a few minutes of jokes. Try to save the very funniest jokes for the end so that the presentation reaches a real climax.

What's black and white and red all over?

A Recipe
for Disaster

Materials: cookbooks or recipes clipped from newspapers and magazines

Point out to the group that a recipe is like a story, with a setting (the kitchen), characters (the ingredients) that go through changes, and a plot with a happy ending (the finished dish). Now read a recipe that players will recognize—pancakes, perhaps. Use tone and pacing to make the recipe into an exciting narrative.

Now invite players to work in pairs to make up their own recipes. Provide them with a few cookbooks for inspiration, but emphasize that the recipes don't have to be ones that would actually work. In fact, the more fanciful they are, the better. Then have partners read their recipes aloud to the group. Encourage players to "serve up" the recipes tastefully and convincingly. They should make the mouth water!

Going Once, Going Twice...

Materials: video of an auction and a way to show it; table; wooden mallet; play money (optional)

Ask players to share what they know about auctions. If necessary, explain that auctions are sales in which customers bid on—or tell how much they are willing to pay for—the objects for sale. The auctioneer displays and describes the objects, and then sells them to the highest bidder. If possible, show a short video of an auction, or perhaps take the group on a field trip to see a real auction. Point out the special mannerisms of auctioneers, especially the lightning quick rhythm of their delivery.

Now have players imagine valuable objects to sell. Each player should think up an item and take notes that describe it. Players will take turns auctioning off their imaginary objects to the group. Point out that players must describe the objects in special detail, since they cannot be seen. Ask players to think about how to sell their objects. What will make them appealing to buyers? What special features do they have? Encourage players to imitate the speech patterns of an auctioneer. Allow a few minutes for bidding on each item. To add to the fun, pass out equal amounts of play money to players before the auction starts. You might even set up an auctioneer's table with a wooden mallet to bang each time an object is sold.

The Secret Tapes

Materials: cassette recorder and blank tapes

Some stories are secret. Invite teams of about four players to imagine they are spies. Their assignment is to make a recording lasting a few minutes with a made-up piece of secret information. What kind of secret? They might tell who stole the jewels and where they can be found, describe a top-secret invention and its uses, or explain a plot to plant a computer virus and how it can be thwarted. Have teams work out their stories together and then put them on tape anonymously. Encourage players to add to the atmosphere by using false names, disguising their voices, creating sound effects, and using lots of difficult or technical words.

Bring the tapes to the following session in a special secret-looking box and bring them out as if they were extremely important documents. Play them for the group and ask: What is the secret about? What helps the tape sound mysterious and exciting? Can you recognize any of the voices?

Ten Random Words

Materials: a newspaper; scissors; a bag or box

This game is very good for warming up or for rounding off a session. In advance, cut ten everyday words from the newspaper—for instance: *evening, hamburger, tickling, 1995, precious stones, nonetheless, bookend, computer, knitting,* and *crying.* Place the words in a box or bag and have ten players each select a word at random. Explain that these players will tell a story together, and each must use his chosen word in the story. Choose a player to begin the story, being sure to include his word. After a couple of sentences, someone else can interrupt and continue the story, putting her own word in. This way players create a short, silly story with a beginning, a middle, and an end. When needed, suggest a switch in storyteller or a change in the course of the story.

If time allows, play the game two or more times and give everyone in the group a turn.

Patchwork Stories

Remind players that every story should have a beginning, a middle, and an end. Divide the group into teams of about three players. Have each team work together to invent a very brief story in three distinct parts. Each team member should choose one story part to tell: beginning, middle, or end.

Now the fun begins. Call on one team to tell their story's beginning. When they finish, choose a different team to tell the middle of their own story. Finally, have a third team tell their story's end. This means that the players have to listen very carefully, since it might be their turn at any moment. Continue until every team has told all three parts of its story. Could the group follow the thread of each story, even though it was broken up? Did any of the stories go particularly well together? Could parts of different stories fit together to form a patchwork story? Invite teams to experiment with combining parts of their stories together.

Back Then

Ask players: What is your earliest childhood memory? Invite each player to recount memories of his childhood home, toys, school, pets, and so on. Many first children will remember the births of siblings. Challenge players to bring the past to life with sensory details, unusual events, and memories of emotions.

My Extraordinary Desk Lamp

Materials: stopwatch

My desk lamp is hardly extraordinary, but I could still talk about it for 5 minutes—and that is the point of this game. Point out to the group that even the most mundane, seemingly uninteresting object has innumerable qualities, uses, and even anecdotes associated with it. Demonstrate by telling about an object you have with you— perhaps a schoolbag. Talk about where you got the bag, why it is useful, what you keep in it, and how you carry it with you all day long. The bag is and remains the main "character" of the story; don't go off on a tangent about the plot of your favorite book, which happens to be in the bag.

Now have players take turns talking about an everyday object for as long as possible. Time players with a stopwatch to see who can go on the longest. Encourage players to keep the audience in mind— they should try to make their stories not only long, but also inter- esting. You may want to set a maximum speaking time, so that no one goes on forever.

Variation: Each player speaks about the same common object. This will show how differently people use and feel about a particular thing. Give the players a week to think and take notes about the object. This will make the content of the stories still richer. During the week, you might mention something about the object each day, or ask a question that will help players to view it in a different light.

Soapbox

Materials: a raised platform, step, or desk that is safe to stand on

Tell players that in the old days people used to stand on soapboxes (or wooden crates) outside the general store to shout their opinions to the town. Point out the platform, step, or desk and explain that this object has been designated as their soapbox for the day.

Invite players to think about any issues they have strong opinions about. How could they express their feelings to the group? Have teams of about four players discuss with each other what they'd like to say and practice their speeches together. Ask players to keep their speeches general, avoiding any personal attacks.

After about 25 minutes of preparation, everyone makes his speech. Don't let players go on too long—about a minute for each speaker should be enough. Pay careful attention so that you can stop any seriously inappropriate speeches before the situation gets out of hand. Periodically you might allow questions or discussion from listeners.

Describe a Painting

Materials: reproductions of abstract paintings from library books, museum postcards, or slides

Display several abstract paintings. Begin the game by picking up one painting and showing it to the group. Tell the group everything the painting suggests to you. You might describe the colors and textures you see, talk about the mood the painting evokes, or tell a story inspired by the image.

Now ask each player to choose one painting and consider what she would like to say about it. Each talk should last about one minute. Setting a time frame encourages the players to say more than just a few words.

Variation: Have players sit in a circle with the pictures spread out in the center. Each player in turn says what he can see in a particular picture without pointing the picture out. Can the group guess which picture he is describing?

Plant a Family Tree

Materials: rulers; markers or crayons; family trees or other genealogical charts (optional)

Display some genealogical charts or draw a simple family tree on the chalkboard—make a trunk ("you") with two branches for the mother and father, four grandparents branching above that, eight great-grandparents branching above that, and so on. Discuss the concepts of genealogy and family trees.

Now divide players into teams of about four players and invite each team to invent a character and his family history. Encourage them to imagine: What is the character's name? Why did his parents give him that name? What are his grandparents like? His great-grandparents? Where did the family come from? What special traditions has the family passed down? What changes have taken place over the years? Teams should brainstorm ideas, make notes on a family tree, and then describe their invented family to the group.

The success of the game relies entirely on the richness of the fantasy created by the players.

Up Tempo

Materials: stopwatch or timer

When talking in front of a group, children are often asked to speak slowly and clearly. In this game, players will have a chance to tell a story as fast as they possibly can. This gives them a chance to explore the effects of tempo on storytelling.

Divide the group into teams of about four players. Each team should choose a story—they might make one up together, or they might choose a fairy tale or the plot of a popular movie. They should divide the story into parts, so that each team member has a part to tell.

Now ask the teams to think of a reason why they have to tell their story very fast. Are they being chased? Do they have to catch a plane? Remind players that their stories should still captivate the audience. After 5 minutes of practice, have teams tell their speedy stories to the whole group while you time them. Which team can tell a complete story the fastest?

Onceuponatimetherewasalittlegirl...

Time Travel

Point out to the group that time is an essential element in a story. Conventionally, the events of a story are told in chronological order, but many stories jump back and forth in time. Movies and TV shows often use "flashbacks" to explain parts of a story.

Choose a story that everyone in the group knows—perhaps a fairy tale, the plot of a popular movie, or a short story that was read in class. Have one player begin telling the story. Soon after, ask her to stop. Choose another player to take up the story, but tell this player to start at a different point in the story, which you choose. For instance: Someone tells the story of an accident; another player continues, but now the time is ten days later. Has the accident victim already left the hospital? If so, where are we now? The player telling the story has to be very quick to imagine the new situation and continue speaking. As the story goes on, keep switching the story-teller and suggesting jumps both forward and backward in time.

Point of View

Point out to the group that one very important part of a story is the voice that tells it. Some stories are narrated by a character, while others have an unnamed, all-knowing narrator. A different narrator can change a story a great deal. In *Confessions of an Ugly Stepsister*, a novel by Gregory Maguire, Cinderella's stepsister tells a very different version of the familiar fairy tale. How might the witch retell "Hansel and Gretel"?

Tell players that in this game, they will work in pairs to tell a story. (Depending on their proficiency, have players retell a familiar story or make up their own.) Each partner will tell the story in the voice of one of the characters. As partners take turns narrating parts of the story, the point of view will keep changing. Remind players that the different characters may disagree with each other about exactly what happened. They might contradict each other and take the story through twists and turns. After pairs have practiced together, ask them to present their stories to the group.

Variations:

- Players might try alternating between taking on the role of a character and acting as an omniscient narrator. In this case, the point of view would change not only in a literary sense but also grammatically: "I" becomes "she" and vice-versa.

- Players could tell a story with multiple characters and take on more than one role each.

Word Games

Words are just sounds in the air or letters on a page, but they are immensely powerful. Words can be soft, sweet, harsh, ugly, strange, or beautiful. They can communicate love or hate, understanding or confusion, truth or lies. Words can create an atmosphere, paint a picture, or dispel an illusion. Words can simply roll off your tongue and may cause you to make awful blunders.

Words in the dictionary seem to be trapped in a static definition; they are locked up in the prison of alphabetical law and order. Fortunately, children don't have to be subject to adult rules. They can make up new words, secret words, and words that have absolutely no meaning, or they can give new meanings to existing words.

This series of games invites players to discuss, picture, identify, create, and play with words.

Vacation Planner

Have players sit in a circle. Begin the game by saying, "I'm leaving on vacation and I'm going to pack my turtle." (Choose any object you like.) Then invite the player to your left to repeat what you said and add an object: "I'm leaving on vacation and I'm going to pack my turtle and my red boots." Going around the circle, each player should repeat the list so far and add a new item of his own. Tell players their words don't have to be objects that anyone would actually take on a trip—encourage them to be inventive.

Variations:

- You might suggest a theme for the packing list, such as: wild animals, well-known people, favorite foods, silly things, or nonsense words.

- Instead of going on vacation, players could be going to school, to bed, or to take a bath. You can think up innumerable variations. Invite players to come up with ideas of their own.

Pet Names

Materials: photos or drawings of animals

Ask players whether they have ever given a name to a new pet, a stuffed animal, or anything else. How do players come up with names? Do they use the names of their favorite stars? Do they describe the animal: Snowball the white rat or Slither the snake? Do they make up nonsense names?

Have players sit in pairs facing each other. One of them holds up a photo or drawing of an animal. The other imagines the animal is her pet and gives it a name. Switch places after a few tries. Then invite players to share the funniest or best names they came up with.

Variation: It's also fun if players write the names down instead of saying them out loud. The pictures can be numbered; one player holds them up, and the other writes down his ideas without showing what he has written. Then partners switch places. When a pair has finished, they can compare lists. Are any names the same or similar?

Word Tennis

Point out to the group that certain words seem to go together. For example, the word *pond* might make someone think of the word *frog*. The word *frog* might make someone think of the word *turtle*. Sometimes word associations are unexpected: The word *turtle* might make someone think of *chocolate*, since there is a kind of chocolate candy called a "turtle."

Have players form pairs and sit facing each other. Explain that the players will take turns calling out words and that each new word should be inspired by the one before it. You might start pairs off with a common word, perhaps if you use the explanation described above. Tell players they can stop the game twice to ask their partners why a certain word made them think of another word. Otherwise, pairs should shoot words back and forth as quickly as they can. After a few minutes, change partners and play again.

 small groups

What's in the Room?

Every room, both at home and at school, has its own particular furnishings. A bed belongs in the bedroom, but a book could be found anywhere and may give no clue as to what room you are in.

Divide the group into teams of about four players. Ask each team to choose a familiar room and make a list of objects found in that room. Then ask team members to think about which objects they have included that could be found anywhere and which could be found only in that room. Have each team read aloud the names of objects from their list while the rest of the group tries to guess which room they belong in. Encourage the team to begin by reading objects that do not give away the exact location of the room, in order to keep the group guessing for as long as possible. How many words can the team read before someone guesses the answer?

Guess the Word

Materials: stopwatch

Invite the group to play a guessing game. Divide the group into two teams. Players should write lots of words on slips of paper, fold them, and place them in one big pile. Explain that players will take turns picking words from the pile and describing them to their team. Players will try to make their team guess each word as quickly as possible, without actually saying the word itself. (For example, a player might describe the word *broccoli* as follows: "This is a green vegetable, shaped like a little tree.") Players can try to think of hard words to challenge the other team, but remind them that they might pick the words themselves.

    Choose a team to go first. Give a player from that team 60 seconds to make his team guess as many words as possible. After 60 seconds are up, the other team takes a turn. Keep going until every player has had a turn describing words. The team with the most slips at the end of the game wins.

Word Diamond

See game 77 (Word Tennis) for an explanation of word associations. On the board, write one word. Invite players to think of two words they associate with the first word. Write these words side by side under the first. Repeat this exercise for each of the two new words. Now call players' attention to one of the pairs of words on the third row. Have them think of one new word that fits with both of those words, and write it underneath. Do the same thing for the other pair of words. Now have players think of one final word that fits with the two words on the fourth row. You will end up with a diamond like this:

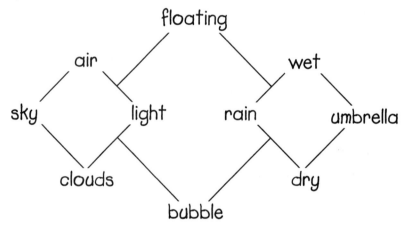

Have players create their own word diamonds. Point out that a word diamond is a nice way of discovering and collecting words since you can easily see how the connections are made. Word diamonds help you make an inventory of what you want to tell or write about.

You might have players use word diamonds to help them get started on a writing or storytelling assignment.

Your Treasure Chest of Words

Materials: markers or crayons; small blank books, either bought or homemade (optional)

Point out to the group that words can be precious. Everyone treasures e-mails from faraway friends, the lyrics of a favorite song, the last sentence of a really good book, or the word *excellent* on a report card. Invite players to think about what words they treasure most. Depending on the group's age and proficiency, have players write a list of twenty to sixty favorite words. Encourage players to think about words that sound beautiful as well as words with meanings they like. Then have players choose the five best words on their lists, write them on a new sheet of paper, and illustrate them. Invite players to display their lists and explain why they chose the words they did.

Variations:

- At the beginning of a semester of classes, have players start their lists in a special notebook or a special section of their notebooks. They can add to the list as the semester goes on, to create an even richer treasury of words.

- Have players bring in or create little blank books to fill with their word treasuries.

82

pairs

What Is
a Football?

Materials: drawing materials (optional)

Tell players that if they stop to think about certain words, they can think up funny new meanings. Is a football a ball with feet or a ball shaped like a foot? Is a treehouse a house where trees live? Is a swimming pool a pool that swims?

After providing a few examples, write several new compound words on the board. You might choose *hot dog, wildflower, shoehorn, childhood, basketball, sheepdog, firefly,* and *mousetrap.* Invite pairs of players to choose words from the board, write funny definitions for them, and illustrate them. Encourage pairs to think up their own words to redefine as well.

After about 20 minutes let the players share their words, definitions, and illustrations with the group. Leave enough time for a lot of laughs!

Variation: Use compound words like the ones above to create a silly multiple-choice quiz. In advance, invent two funny alternative meanings for each word. Include the correct definition as well. Have players choose definition A, B, or C for each word on the quiz.

Kind Words

Explain that this game is about thinking, breathing, and reacting. Divide the group into pairs. Tell players they will take turns paying each other compliments—note that the compliments shouldn't be based on reality, but entirely made up. Before a player replies to what his partner has said, he first takes a deep breath and thinks about it. Only then does he react with another word or phrase, even more complimentary than his partner's. Encourage players to begin with ordinary words and build up to a ridiculous level of exaggerated compliments.

Variation: You could play the game above with a different type of progression: For example, partners could exchange words or phrases that are increasingly hot, cold, scared, or sad.

Homophone Lines

Materials: joke books containing puns (optional)

Write the following pairs of words on the board: *I/eye, hole/whole,* and *blue/blew*. Point out that some words (homophones) sound exactly the same but have different spellings and meanings. Help players brainstorm a list of homophones and write them on the board. (Kids' joke books containing puns may help give players ideas.) Have each player choose a pair of words and write sentences using each word in context. Then have them switch the homophones in the two sentences. For example, a player might end up with:

The rat had a long **tale**.

Everyone listened to his **tail**.

Help players come up with homophone pairs and sentences that will result in silly incongruities. Now the fun begins. Have players take a new sheet of paper and fold it in half. On each side, have them illustrate one of the mixed-up sentences, without writing the words. Players can exchange papers and try to guess what homophone pair is shown.

Matrix Language

On a chalkboard or large easel, write the word *flower* in "matrix language." This involves drawing a flower by writing the names of its various parts. First write the word *stem* vertically, then add the word *leaf* curling on either side, and write *petal* four or five times radiating from the top of the stem. You might even add *pistil* and *stamen* between the petals. If possible, the drawing should be identifiable by shape, and the words should also be legible.

Invite players to try writing words in this "matrix language." How can they write words like *cat, tree,* or *house*? When players have finished, have them display their "matrix words."

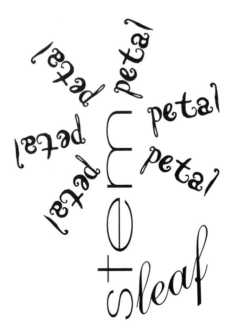

Story-Writing Games

Faced with the task of writing a story, many people have no idea how to begin. The element of play can be the spark that sets creativity ablaze. These games invite players to approach writing in a fun, playful, low-pressure environment. As leader, make sure you emphasize the creative process rather than the result. Try not to place too much focus on correct punctuation or spelling mistakes. Do your best to nurture rather than squelch the enthusiasm of potential writers.

Create an inviting setting for writing. Make sure there is plenty of paper available, as well as a variety of writing implements. You may wish to experiment with seating arrangements: You might place desks in a circle or rectangle or even have players lounge on the floor (for short writing games). It also helps enormously if the space is clean, comfortable, and pleasantly decorated. Players can write in blank books or spiral notebooks. Ask players to write clearly so that the texts can be passed around the group.

The section About Composing Stories on page 6 will help you walk a group through the steps involved in creating a story. The games in this section give players opportunities to explore story elements further.

A **Fish** out of **Water**

Invite players to imagine an animal who wishes she were something else. Maybe a snake desperately wants to be a dog, and goes around wagging its tail, fetching sticks in its fangs, and trying to learn how to bark ("ssswooofsss"). Players might invent catlike hippos, bunny-like crocodiles, bearish monkeys, piggy elephants, and so on. Have players write stories about their animals. The only condition is that the animal remains in his usual environment so that the contrasts are immediately apparent in the story. After 25 minutes have players read their stories aloud.

Variations:

- Invite players to imagine that their animals try so hard to be different that they begin to resemble other animals. For instance, a pig who wants so badly to be an elephant that his nose begins to grow and his legs thicken into trunks.

- Have players illustrate their stories with drawings of animals who have the outer features of other animals: for instance, a hippo-cat.

- Have players write about animals who want to be human.

Cartoon Balloons

Materials: cardboard; scissors; thick markers

First session:

In advance, prepare a sheet of paper for every player in the group. At the top of each sheet, write an exclamation, a question, or a short sentence. Each of these will form the first line of a dialog. To begin

the game, have players sit in a circle. Pass out the dialog sheets. Have each player add a line of dialog to the sheet and pass it to the player on her left. Each sheet should go around in this manner until it returns to the player it started with. Ask players to write a closing sentence for their dialogs. Now have players form pairs to work on the dialogs. Partners should read aloud and revise the dialogs and choose one to act out.

Second session:

Help pairs cut large, cartoon-style "speech balloons" out of cardboard. Partners should write each line of their dialog in thick marker on one balloon. Then have the pairs combine to form teams of four to perform the dialogs for the group. As one pair silently acts out its dialog, the other pair will hold the speech balloons over the actors' heads. The actors should mime expressions and gestures that support the speech balloons over their heads.

Upside-down Stories

Begin telling a story to players in which black is white, day is night, and the world is turned upside-down. For example, time could go backwards, dogs could own humans and walk them on leashes, or kids could rule the world.

Invite players to think of their own "upside-down" stories. Encourage them to use their imaginations and come up with outlandish scenarios. After 30 minutes, the stories from the switched-around world are read aloud. This game stimulates players' creativity and sense of humor so that they learn to view reality in a different light. Children, in particular, love to turn the world around.

Relay Story

Have players sit in a circle or in a line. At the top of a sheet of paper, write one intriguing sentence that forms the beginning of a story. Pass the paper to the first player and ask her to add a sentence of her own telling what happened next. The story goes from player to player, getting longer and longer. Have the last player read the story aloud.

Variation: Have players sit in a circle, each with a sheet of paper and a pen. Each player should write one sentence to begin a story. The papers pass round the whole circle (as above) and end up with the one who wrote the first line. Then have players take turns reading the stories aloud.

Musical Notes

Materials: music cassettes or CDs and a player

In advance, choose a favorite piece of music, preferably one without words, to play for the group. (See suggestions below.) Point out to the group that different kinds of music call up different emotions and feelings. Music may stir the imagination, energize us, relax us, or disturb us.

Tell players that you will play music, and they should write down their thoughts as they listen. Players could write in phrases or sentences, or simply make a list of words. Encourage players to write as many words as they can. Tell them they don't need to worry about creating a perfect piece of writing. When the music ends, invite volunteers to share some of what they have written.

Note: Here are a few suggestions for music to inspire writing: "Gymnopédies/Gnossiennes" by Erik Satie, film music by Michael Nyman ("The Piano"), "Nocturnes" by Frederic Chopin, music by Igor Stravinsky, "Passion" by Peter Gabriel, "Labyrinth" by Trevor Jones and David Bowie, "Atom Heart Mother" by Pink Floyd, and "The Last Emperor" by Ryuichi Sakamoto and David Byrne.

Good Versus Evil

In many stories, good battles evil. Have pairs of players work together to create a hero and a villain. On two sheets of paper, they list the characteristics and secret wishes of the two characters. Encourage players to tell each character's

- name
- age
- gender
- personality traits
- appearance
- job
- likes and dislikes
- ambitions (schemes? evil plots?)
- abilities (any special powers?)

Hang up the pages when they are finished. Players can then choose a few heroes and villains and write their own stories of good versus evil.

Change the Character's Character

This game focuses on how a character's personality affects a story. Characters should not be featureless heroes and villains who simply react to situations: A character's personality can be the driving force in a story, creating complications and opening doors to resolutions. How might the story of "Little Red Riding Hood" be different if the title character were a tough, no-nonsense kickboxer? In this game, players will find out.

Write the following five personality types on the board (or make up a few of your own):

- a person who is melancholy and feels that life has no meaning

- a person who revels in eating and drinking and does everything for pleasure

- a person who is self-important and has no time to stop and smell the roses

- a person who is tough and takes no nonsense from anyone

- a joker who never takes anything seriously

Divide the group into teams of about four players. Choose a story that is familiar to everyone (a short story read in a previous class, a fairy tale, or the plot of a popular movie). Tell the teams that they will work together to rewrite the story, giving the main character the personality traits of one of the five types on the board. Ask

teams to have the character narrate the story as v
ample opportunity for the character's personality
Point out that the different personality types will in
a great deal. Teams should feel free to change the
story if their character's personality dictates it. When
finished, have the teams read them aloud. Let the grou
differences. People with different characters experien
events in completely different ways. One person might ha. uly notice
something that is immensely important to another.

Example: If Little Red Riding Hood were a person who lives for
pleasure, she would almost certainly go into great detail about all
the delicious things her mother put into the basket. Perhaps she
would get carried away and eat most of the goodies and have to ask
the wolf for help in getting more....

What Could Possibly Go Wrong?

Tell players that an essential part of creating a story is building up tension. The characters must encounter a conflict, or too little will happen. Divide the group into teams of three or four players. Have each team member think up a happy, good situation—a rafting trip through the Grand Canyon, a group of friends who put on plays together, a land where violence and disease have been magically abolished—and describe it in a few sentences at the top of a sheet of paper.

Then have the teammates rotate papers. Players should take the ideal situation their teammate described at the top of the page and think of what could go wrong. Have them write in a few sentences what problem the characters could encounter.

Now have teammates rotate papers one more time, so that each player gets a sheet he has not yet seen. In a few sentences, have players write a solution or possible outcome to the problem described on the paper. Finally, ask teammates to read their papers aloud to one another and discuss the situations, conflicts, and resolutions they have come up with. If players like an idea, they might use it as the basis of a story.

The **D-Story**

Materials: dictionaries

Invite players to write a story of about ten lines in which all the main words (nouns, verbs, adverbs, adjectives) begin with the letter *d*. For example:

> The detective decoded a diagram directing her downriver to the disappeared diadem decorated with diamonds. Docking her dory, she dived down into the dank depths. Descending, she dodged dolphins and damselfish darting daintily. Down in the debris, she decided to dig. Despite the dimness, she discerned dots of dancing daylight delineating a diadem.... Deceived! The devious desperado had deposited a dummy diadem decorated with dimes, not diamonds. Duped by a decoy!

Each player makes a list of words beginning with *d*. Dictionaries and books of word games can be a great help. Tell players that they can link the words of their story with short words that don't begin with *d*, such as *a, the, and, but, or, he, she, in, on,* and so on. All nouns and verbs must begin with *d*, however. Point out that strange sentences are unavoidable and that the story does not have to be strictly logical. You may wish to suggest a title if players need ideas. Give players a chance to write a draft and revise it. After half an hour, invite players to read their stories.

Variations:

- You can, of course, choose another letter. Almost any letter besides *q, x,* and *z* should yield stories without too much difficulty. For variety, you might try having each player choose a different letter.

- Have players write an alliterative poem. For this variation, have players use exclusively words beginning with the chosen letter (no *but, the, she,* and so on).

Idea Bank

Materials: notecards; a box in which to keep the notecards

Tell players they are going to create a bank—not a bank for money, but a bank for story ideas. Have each player come up with an idea for a story and summarize it on a notecard. Then have each player create three more cards for the story: On one they describe the story's beginning, on another they write about a conflict or problem the characters face in the middle of the story, and on the third they describe the story's ending. Players should keep their summary card and deposit the other three cards in the story bank. If players have ideas for multiple stories, encourage them to create story cards for all of them. Ideally, the bank should have 100 or so cards inside.

When the bank is ready, have each player select one card. If a player picks her own card, she should put it back and choose a new one. Players use the idea on the card (for a story's beginning, middle, or ending) as the seed for a complete story of their own. If a player is unable to work with a particular card, he can exchange it for another. Players write their stories and then read them aloud. Can listeners recognize stories that were inspired by the cards they wrote?

After the game is over, encourage players to add to the idea bank when inspiration strikes and to use it whenever they need ideas.

Variation: Have players create cards describing the story's setting, its main characters, and a problem the characters must solve. If you color-code the cards, players can select one of each for a mix-and-match story plan.

Poetry Games

Many people think poems must rhyme, contain flowery language, deal with exalted subjects, and be very difficult to write. These games help players understand that writing a poem can be as simple as jotting down what they see, hear, smell, taste, and feel on an ordinary day. Every poem grows out of a thought.

This series of games helps players put their everyday feelings and experiences on paper. Most of the games are writing assignments, but they can also be read aloud or acted out for the group.

Concentration, respect for each other, and a pleasant, open atmosphere are essential for poetry writing. See the introduction to the story-writing games on page 106 for suggestions on how to create such an atmosphere.

on your
own

Collect Your Thoughts

Suggest to the group a subject or theme—"spring" or "snow," for instance. Younger children may need a short discussion on the subject to clarify the assignment. Ask players to make a word list relating to the subject under discussion. Players can write down any words that come into their heads. They should feel free to include phrases and short sentences on their lists.

Now have players write out ten thoughts on the subject. What does spring (or whatever subject you have chosen) mean to them? When players have written their thoughts, invite them to jot words from their list next to the ideas associated with them. Have players cross out words they can't use. Then ask them to arrange the remaining concepts in an order that feels right to them and explain that they will next be creating a poem using these concepts. Players can go through this cutting and rearranging process again, but encourage them to write a poem that uses at least five of their original ideas. When the poems are complete, invite players to read them aloud.

Variation: As players revise their poems, encourage them to repeat a line or a thought if they want to give it particular emphasis. Ask: Which idea is the most important to you? How can you show its importance?

Hidden Word Poems

Ask each player to choose a word (with five or more letters) that could form the basis of a poem. Players might choose their own names, the names of their pets or hometown, favorite foods, or ideas such as *friendship*. Have each player write his chosen word in capital letters down the left edge of a sheet of paper. Now he should use each letter of the word to begin a line of his poem.

When the poems are finished, you might invite players to read them aloud and ask the group to guess the word that inspired each poem. (Have players indicate each time they begin a new line, so the group can keep track of the initial letters.)

Example:

Sunshine beaming from your face

Makes me warm inside

Ice cream couldn't be as sweet

Lips curling up like licorice whips

Eyes crinkling at the edges like candy wrappers

Diamond Poems

As in game 96 (Collect Your Thoughts), have players write word lists about a subject. Explain that players will choose just 16 words and arrange them in a diamond shape to create a poem. Write the following example (or one like it) on the board:

Sun

lounging on

a beach towel

how wonderful it is!

what is that?

a cloud?

rain!

Point out the pattern for the number of words on each line: 1, 2, 3, 4, 3, 2, 1. All together, this adds up to 16 words. Now invite players to choose 16 words and to create their own diamond poems. Encourage them to think about how to build their poems: Will they introduce the subject with the first word or keep the reader guessing? Will they describe an event, give an opinion, or air feelings? Will they use the final word to sum up the poem or retain an air of mystery?

When the poems are complete, invite players to write them on the board and read them aloud. Make sure players do not read too quickly.

Name Rap

This is a short game to help players understand the rhythm of words. Use players' names as an example: Point out names that have one syllable, two syllables, three syllables, and so on. Then invite players to think about which syllable of each name is stressed, or given emphasis. Is it the first syllable (Ashley) or the second syllable (Rasheed)? Explain that some poems have regular rhythms—for example, alternating stressed and unstressed syllables. Challenge the group to string players' names together to form regular rhythms that can be chanted and clapped:

Lashauna, Marco, Max, Renée

Alison, Seneca, Lisa, and Ling

How many different rhythms can they come up with?

Variation: Challenge players to make their strings of names rhyme as well.

Note: Make sure players understand that a piece of writing does not have to have a regular rhythm or rhyme scheme to make it qualify as poetry.

Haiku
Arguments

Materials: one or two examples of haiku

A haiku is a Japanese form of poem consisting of three lines of five, seven, and five syllables. Before introducing haiku, you may wish to use game 99 (Name Rap) to review the concept of syllables. If possible, show the group a few examples of traditional haiku that have been translated into English. Players may notice that haiku often celebrate nature.

Tell players that they will write their own haiku. Ask them to begin with a statement, answer with a contradiction, and conclude with a surprise. For instance:

> What a lovely day!
> Don't you feel the soaking rain?
> Water feeds the heart.

> I feel energized.
> The baby cried all night long!
> His scream is music.

The players now write their own haiku and read them aloud.

The Same Beginning

Materials: newspaper article

Simplicity can add power to a poem. A poem that expresses an opinion using lines that all begin with the same phrase can be fascinating.

Example:

> I don't know any kids who are lost
>
> I don't know any kids without homes
>
> I don't know any kids without enough to eat
>
> I don't know yet how to help those in need
>
> I don't know how much longer I can go on not helping

Read aloud a newspaper story that will get the group thinking. You might choose a story about poverty, corruption, discrimination, or another example of unfairness in the world. Ask players to write a poem about their thoughts on the issue. Tell them that every line of the poem should start with the same words. You might suggest an opening phrase for players to use. After 20 minutes, have players read their thought poems. Give them a chance to discuss the issues raised and possible solutions to the problems they wrote about.

The Games Arranged According to Age Groups

Young Children
(K-Grade 2)

1. Letter Collages
2. Letter Hunt
3. Find the Letters
4. Letterbox
5. Explore a World of Letters
6. Morphing Letters
7. Letter Pictures
8. Read My Lips
26. Feeling Words
31. When I Grow Up...
32. Group Cheer
42. Voice Tricks
43. What Sound Does a Fridge Make?
44. A Story with Sound Effects
45. If Animals Could Talk
46. A Noise in the Dark
47. Not a Bangbangbang, a Zzzzt-zzzzzt
48. Sound Boxes
58. A Story Full of Holes
75. Vacation Planner
76. Pet Names

Elementary School Children (K-Grade 5)

26. Feeling Words
31. When I Grow Up...
32. Group Cheer
46. A Noise in the Dark
47. Not a Bangbangbang, a Zzzzt-zzzzzt
48. Sound Boxes

58. A Story Full of Holes
76. Pet Names

Older Children
(Grades 3-5)

9. Letters in Action
10. Sign Language
12. The Same Word
13. The Singing Paper
14. Words Inside Words
15. Clipping the Headlines
16. Headline Scramble
17. Headline Puzzles
18. Ad-lib Ads
19. Photo Finish
20. Good News or Bad News?
21. What Happened Next?
25. Hearing Words
26. Feeling Words
27. Eat Your Words
28. Let the Mood Move You
29. I Hear the Waves Crashing
31. When I Grow Up...
32. Group Cheer
33. Matchmaker
34. Do You Like Liver?
35. Q&A
36. Nice to Meet You
37. My Favorite Word
38. We the Players...
46. A Noise in the Dark
47. Not a Bangbangbang, a Zzzzt-zzzzzt
48. Sound Boxes
49. Consonants and Vowels
50. Sounds of the Body

Older Children and Adolescents (Grades 3-8)

Older Children, Adolescents, and Teens (Grades 3-12)

Adolescents in Middle School

(Grades 6-8)

Teens in High School

(Grades 9-12)

Adolescents in Middle School and Teens in High School

(Grades 6-12)

All Ages

More *SmartFun* Activity Books
for ages 4 and up

The SmartFun activity books encourage imagination, social interaction, and self-expression in children. Games are organized by the skills they develop and marked for appropriate age levels, times of play, and group size. Most games are noncompetitive and require no special skills or training. The series is widely used in homes, schools, day-care centers, clubs, and summer camps.

101 MUSIC GAMES FOR CHILDREN: Fun and Learning with Rhythm and Song by Jerry Storms

All you need to play these 101 music games are music tapes or CDs and simple instruments, many of which kids can have fun making from common household items. Many games are especially good for large group settings, such as birthday parties and day-care. Others are easily adapted to meet classroom needs. No musical knowledge is required.

Over 200,000 copies sold in 11 languages worldwide

160 pages ... 30 illus. ... Paperback $12.95 ... Spiral bound $17.95

101 MORE MUSIC GAMES FOR CHILDREN: New Fun and Learning with Rhythm and Song *by* Jerry Storms

This action-packed compendium offers ingenious song and dance activities from a variety of cultures. These help children enjoy themselves while developing a love for music. Besides listening, concentration, and expression games, this book includes rhythm games, dance and movement games, relaxation games, card and board games, and musical projects.

192 pages ... 72 illus. ... Paperback $12.95 ... Spiral bound $17.95

101 DANCE GAMES FOR CHILDREN: Fun and Creativity with Movement *by* Paul Rooyackers

The games in this book combine movement and play in ways that encourage children to interact and express how they feel in creative fantasies and without words. They are organized into meeting and greeting games, cooperation games, story dances, party dances, "musical puzzles," dances with props, and more. No dance training or athletic skills are required.

160 pages ... 30 illus. ... Paperback $12.95 ... Spiral bound $17.95

For more information visit www.hunterhouse.com

101 DRAMA GAMES FOR CHILDREN: Fun and Learning with Acting and Make-Believe *by* Paul Rooyackers

These noncompetitive games include introduction games, sensory games, pantomime games, story games, sound games, games with masks, games with costumes, and many more. The "play-ful" ideas in *101 Drama Games for Children* help to develop creativity and self-esteem, improvisation, communication, and trust.

160 pages ... 30 illus. ... Paperback $12.95 ... Spiral bound $17.95

101 MOVEMENT GAMES FOR CHILDREN: Fun and Learning with Playful Moving *by* Huberta Wiertsema
August 2002

These games include variations on old favorites such as "Duck, Duck, Goose" as well as new games such as "Mirroring," "Equal Pacing," and "Moving Joints."

101 MORE DRAMA GAMES FOR CHILDREN: New Fun and Learning with Acting and Make-Believe
by Paul Rooyackers   *August 2002*

Includes improvisational games that encourage total involvement and cooperation from participants and offer a wealth of possibilities for play sessions.

UPCOMING BOOKS IN THIS SERIES...

101 MORE DANCE GAMES FOR CHILDREN: New Fun and Creativity with Movement
by Paul Rooyackers   *November 2002*

Introductory Games, Animal Dance Games, Character Dance Games, Street Dance Games, Dance a Story, Dancing with Props, and Dance Notations.

YOGA GAMES FOR CHILDREN: Fun and Fitness with Postures, Movements and Breath
by Danielle Bersma and Marjoke Visscher   *November 2002*

A playful introduction to yoga for children ages 6–12. The games help young people develop body awareness, physical strength, and flexibility. The 54 exercises are variations on traditional yoga exercises, adjusted for children.

All books $12.95 paperback, $17.95 spiral bound

All prices subject to change